Scale Up!

The Founders' Guide to Accelerating Growth by Building Dream Teams

Sarah Bishop

Scale Up!

The Founders' Guide to Accelerating Growth by Building Dream Teams

ISBN: 9781068188701 Paperback

Published by: Inspired By Publishing

Dedication

To all the entrepreneurs who dare to dream big and the teams that help turn those dreams into reality. Here's to helping you sleep better at night so you can carry on dreaming!

Dedication

[illegible]

Acknowledgements

To my very supportive wife, Katja, who was largely ignored while I was running around for the Your Doctor Film & Media (YDFM) project, which provided so much experience and learning curves in such a short amount of time. She endured holidays where I would "just pop off to interview a few CEOs or Client Relationship Managers," and instead of moaning about it, she simply started playing "guess which candidate will land the role," taking a real interest in what was going on. She has provided a home life (despite my bouncing between our home in Vienna and work in the UK) that has enabled me to sit and write this book, between recruiting, training and coaching projects that I juggle in my AuDHD-fueled quest for dopamine and difference. I truly believe that this is partly what makes me a bit of a Swiss Army Knife of recruitment and useful in all kinds of situations.

To Vanessa Di Cuffa, a People and Culture professional extraordinaire and a very dear friend, for introducing me to her brother, the founder of YDFM, Dr. Riccardo Di Cuffa, and his CEO, Peter Watts, who all trusted me to come through with their growth plans. Even when there weren't any plans!

To Becky Bishop, Claire Reece-Poole and Kerry Greenland, who are all very fine recruiters. I am privileged to have them as professional partners, and even more so, to consider them family and friends. They worked like Trojans to find, interview, and support candidates for critical roles on tight deadlines.

My marvellous Marianne Carter, who handles our social media presence, operational support and basically anything that's thrown at her, for which I am truly grateful. Marianne is much more than an employee. I consider her a treasured friend, and she has proven to be a loyal and supportive constant through both the good and bad times at Recruit Recruit Ltd. I love our Tuesday and Friday catch-ups where we probably talk more nonsense than strategy, laugh about really silly stuff, and then get on with it.

To all the fantastic candidates who took a leap of faith, embraced the chaos and uncertainty of start-up life, and helped to shape it into a successful and exciting business that delivered results. They played their part in keeping all our favourite shows, series, and films on the tellybox and streaming services while we all festered away at home during the pandemic lockdowns. People like Laura Jackson, Sam Dunham, Sergei Mitoi (some of the very first employees), and Katie Gallop (a phenomenal senior HR professional) became key drivers of delivery and operational success within the business very quickly, under demanding and ever-changing circumstances.

Finally, to everyone at Inspired By Publishing for getting this thing to print! Especially founder Chloe Bisson, who inspired (see what I did there?) me with her story while speaking on stage at an Expert Empires event, and Angela Haynes-Ranger. Angela has been my Author Mentor and Project Manager and has been the most patient, encouraging, calming influence, and well-needed accountability partner to get my book written. She has been completely unflappable and unsurprised, as I wove from three to five months behind schedule to suddenly catching everything up within the space of a few weeks, thus dumping a shit-ton of work on her in one go!

Contents

Introduction

Most entrepreneurs start their businesses with some sort of growth in mind.

You may have gone it alone to increase your earning potential or simply do a better job than the one your previous employer allowed you to do. After a time, you find yourself bored with "working on the tools" or doing really well and ready to grow the business. You may be driven by a mission or purpose and want to grow to reach as many people as possible. Or you may have set out with massive ambitions from the outset and are obsessed with finding your unicorn!

Whether it's the mythical start-up with billions of turnover potential or that elusive genius hire who'll magically solve all your problems, there is one thing they don't tell you about unicorns: Unicorns are overrated. In fact, I'd argue they don't even exist (in business, that is. I firmly believe in real unicorns with rainbow manes and glittery farts!). What you really need is a team of misfits – yes, the ones who didn't get picked first in the proverbial school sports team. Because when you're building something from nothing, it's not about finding one perfect person; it's about building a team of imperfect but brilliant humans who fit together like a strange, puzzle-solving superpower.

Like most people in the recruitment industry, I fell into it rather than consciously decided on it as a career move. I mean, no child dreams of being a Recruitment Consultant when they grow up. I really wanted to be a Blue Peter presenter, Bugsy Malone or a vet. But by the time I went off to University, I wanted to be the next David Attenborough. After studying Environmental Science, I realised that I was probably too loud and swear-y to be Attenborough or on children's television. All the jobs in conservation and environmental management, back in the 1990s, had salaries that would leave me with student loan repayments into my nineties. So, with all my lofty ideals and convictions flying out the window, I decided to get a sales job. My plan was to earn loads of commission, pay off all my student debt, and then march off to Africa to save the elephants, as I'd told my old Headteacher I would do when she demanded, somewhat exasperated with my efforts to entertain the school rather than pass my A levels, "What on earth do you intend on doing with your life?

Spoiler alert: I never got to Africa to save the elephants. The closest I came was a charity trek through the Great Rift Valley in Kenya in 2003 and regularly supporting WWF (nature charity, not the wrestling organisation!) projects.

I also have AuDHD. It's like regular ADHD with a scoop of high-functioning autism thrown in. Although it has its challenges, I also believe that my neurodiversity is one of the reasons I excelled in sales and recruitment. We're very good at being social chameleons. The desire to fit in and not seem so weird all the time means that we often develop this ability to model and mask. It's exhausting, but it makes us quite adaptable in any group or one-to-one scenario. It can be confusing to others (and ourselves) because we quickly and intuitively get the measure of people while often missing other social cues. We then rationalise our gut reaction away, only to find we were right in the first instance – but that's probably for another book. What it does mean is that I have spent most of my life, both unconsciously and consciously, studying human behaviour, communication, and rapport. Combine that with formal training in sales, interviewing, psychology, and neuro-linguistic programming (NLP), and you have a well-rounded skill set for dealing with people.

In the following pages, I'm going to tell you how I helped a start-up grow from a pandemic-induced need to £30 million in revenue in 21 short (and often insane) months. Spoiler: The secret isn't hiring the so-called "best." It's hiring the right ones, and that's a whole different game. I'm going to give you the strategies and tools you need to grow the teams that will scale your business and help you realise your dream.

Whichever camp you fall in, there is something in here for you. Unless you have no intention of growing your business beyond you – in that case, send the book back and ask for a refund! If you intend to do everything yourself (without outsourcing any aspect of the business) until the day you wind it all down after working all those years, this isn't for you. For the rest of you, whether your ambitions are huge and you have funding or investment, or the growth plan is more modest and you're bootstrapping it, you will find tips and tactics that you can implement in your business to facilitate growth.

I cover everything from how you outline a strategy and identify what and who you need to hire at each stage of growth, to how you find, select and secure those talented individuals who will drive your success. It would be remiss not to include how you select and work with the right recruiters to deliver the best results, or how you create your own talent acquisition team if you want to do it yourself, as a professional recruiter. Once you have all the parts in place, or outsource the right bits to the right people, you will start to find you have fewer plates to spin. You will see your stress and frustration levels reduce. You'll be able to sleep better at night and focus on growing your business instead of being sucked into all the doing. You'll be creating a support structure for yourself, as well as a team of people who share your vision, understand your mission, and will help carry the load. Most importantly, you will be on your way to achieving the time and financial freedom you crave, allowing you to pursue what is truly important to you. The best time to read this book is as soon as you have the idea that you're going to start your own business. The second-best time is now.

I wrote this book because I am tired of seeing stressed-out entrepreneurs and founders who are frustrated and unable to scale as planned, as they are overwhelmed by all their to-dos. I wrote it because there are so many failed businesses that could have been success stories if only they had had the right people on board at the earliest opportunity. I wrote it because my own business could be much bigger and more successful had I followed the advice I give my clients. How many of you are really great at sorting other people's problems out, only to find yourself facing them in your own life? Me too. I'm not super-human and I'm not infallible. I'm also not super-wealthy and have not yet reached my own financial and time freedom goals. I'm closer, no doubt. And I could have been there five or ten years ago if I had followed all the stuff that I'm laying out for you here.

So, why should you listen to me if I haven't yet achieved these lofty ambitions myself? Quite simply, because I have helped others to do it. Multiple times. I know! I'm a genius! Yet, if I had followed my own advice from day one and achieved all I set out to, I wouldn't have had the learning curve and experiences that have informed me in ways that enable me to share a much more rounded and effective approach with you now. I wouldn't have the scars, war stories and awareness of the pitfalls and counter-intuitive moves necessary to garner success. This book would be an ideal world scenario, and we all know we don't live in an ideal world.

I've spent 29 years in the trenches of the recruitment industry at the time of writing. I have worked across a variety of sectors and disciplines, recruiting for micro businesses, SMEs, corporates, and the public sector. I started as a trainee recruitment consultant, placing office-based commercial temporary workers, and worked through various roles before becoming the Head of Corporate Sales and Public Sector Division. The company I worked with for 13 years was very entrepreneurial, and I was payroll number 33. I believe the turnover was around £5 million or more when I joined. When I left, it was c. £101M and c. £380M when they sold to JobandTalent in 2021. I witnessed firsthand and contributed to impressive growth in a very competitive market over the years.

While working at Extra Personnel/The Staffing Group, I was part of several teams that worked on some large-volume recruitment campaigns for growing businesses. These included companies that became instantly recognisable brands such as Phones4U, HomeServe, and the Holiday Hypermarket. The projects primarily focused on staffing the call centres. This was a fairly homogeneous recruitment exercise. Hundreds of call centre operatives are placed with the odd team leader or managerial role thrown in. Through my own business, Recruit Recruit, I've had the privilege of working with businesses that require a more diverse mix of skills and experience to round out their senior leadership teams and/or create all the support teams and functions that any successful business needs. This extends to much more than simply filling vacancies that are submitted and requires a whole different level of engagement, knowledge, and strategic input.

I've long been miffed about the job title Recruitment Consultant. The majority don't consult in the slightest. They fill orders. Some do it better than others, but few ask, "Is this actually what you need in your business right now?" before moving on to find suitable candidates. Many people don't know who they really need to hire in the early stages of growth, leading to avoidable and costly hiring mistakes. But why is it so important to get it right early on? Because getting the wrong people in place early on can stifle your growth and send your stress levels skyrocketing. At worst, it will cause your business to fail. You may be thinking, I don't need to hire anyone just yet. Whether you think you're too small now or you've just secured a few million in funding and think your first priority should be to invest it all in the product or service development and delivery, then think again.

Facebook started out as a means for Harvard students to connect and communicate with one another. Not a huge market. Yet Mark Zuckerberg wasn't the only person involved from the beginning. There were five founders. Mainly because it's impossible to do it all yourself (with any decent results) while trying to study or having a life outside of work. By the time they launched as The Facebook in 2004, they had seven employees. In 2005, they had 15. There were 150 employees by 2006 and 450 by 2007. Make no mistake, these are the people who helped grow Facebook and the Metaverse. Mark Zuckerberg, Eduardo Saverin, Andrew McCollum, Dustin Moskovitz, and Chris Hughes were the ideas guys who started the ball rolling and did the early operational stuff. It is physically impossible for the company to have grown to the behemoth it is now if they had tried to do it all themselves for too long.

There are currently over 67,000 Metaverse employees.

Now, while you may not be hankering to grow the next Facebook or a company that is anywhere near that size, you can recognise that you cannot achieve the level of time, financial freedom, or impact that you set out to achieve, all alone. This book will show you how you don't have to be alone.

Some of you may be thinking, I'd rather be alone than have to deal with other people and their drama or demands on my time. Or that other people will create more work for you. And this can happen if you get the wrong people in at the wrong time. I'll show you how to avoid that. Trust me. He did...

"Recruit Recruit enabled us to move effectively and efficiently from a single employee to over 220 in less than 20 months as we moved quickly through the gears from start-up to a £30M turnover business. We could not have done this without them."

– Peter Watts, Group CEO, Your Doctor Holdings Ltd

And now, I'll walk you through the strategies you'll need that will allow you to realise your dreams.

Chapter 1
The Importance of Having a People Strategy

Let's face it, most of us didn't start our businesses dreaming about org charts and HR policies. We were too busy imagining our products flying off the shelves or our services changing the world. But here's the kicker: Without the right people strategy, those dreams are about as likely to come true as me winning the Olympic gold in synchronised swimming – trust me, you don't want to see that!

Why You Need a People Strategy (Even If You Think You Don't)

You might have started your business to boost your earning potential or do a better job than your previous employer allowed. Maybe you're driven by a grand mission. Perhaps you've been working solo and are now ready to expand, or you've had massive ambitions from day one. Whatever your motivation, there comes a point when you realise that to grow, you need more than just yourself.

Now, I know what you're thinking: "I'll just hire an all-rounder!" You know, that mythical unicorn who can do it all. Well, I hate to break it to you, but unicorns are overrated. In fact, they don't even exist (in business, that is – I'm still holding out hope for the ones with rainbow manes and glittery farts). What you really need is a team of misfits. Yes, the ones who didn't get picked first in school sports. Because when you're building something from nothing, it's not about finding one perfect person; it's about building a team of imperfect but brilliant humans who fit together like a strange, puzzle-solving superpower.

Without a strategy, you're going to hire reactively and create problems for yourself further down the line. You're going to make rash decisions because you'll be trying to hire when you're at your busiest and most stressed. You'll find sticking plaster fixes rather than long-term solutions, and you will pay dearly for it in terms of time and energy, unless you are very lucky. You will possibly be tempted to rope in friends and family at the early stages. For every success story where this approach has worked, there are several instances of broken families and friendships where one or more parties have been unable to separate their business and personal lives and decisions.

The People Strategy Is Your Secret Weapon for Scaling Success

A solid people strategy is your blueprint for assembling this dream team. It's not just HR jargon; it's a thoughtful approach to managing and empowering your most valuable asset – your employees. Think of it as the secret sauce that will help you in all areas of your business.

A people strategy will help align your team with your business goals, ensuring everyone pulls in the same direction. It will make sure you map out the skills you need, when you need them, rather than panicking and making reactive hires when you're at your busiest. It will facilitate your plan for growth and succession so that you drive it rather than it driving (or sucking the life out of) you. A solid people strategy helps you manage performance without awkward (and often ineffective) annual reviews. Once you've mapped what and who you need, where and when you're likely to need them, it is also easier to develop your team's skills. This means you can offer development plans, progression and promotion, which aids retention and loyalty in the workforce.

For me, one of the most important aspects of a good people strategy is that it allows you to cultivate your leadership team, so you're not stuck doing everything forever, and you're not just hiring more and more direct reports to manage.

In my experience, most founders and business owners get this arse backwards, and only think of having a people strategy when things start getting complicated and messy. If at all!

We often spend so much time thinking and worrying about how we're going to make things happen that we forget to consider *who* can make those things happen.

You can utilise various proven methods to shape your strategy, or you can start from scratch and develop your own ideas. I firmly believe that emulating a tried and tested strategy is a quicker route to success. Why reinvent the wheel, right?

This is demonstrated nicely in Daniel Priestley's approach to growing his businesses. For those unfamiliar with Dan's work, he is a serial entrepreneur and author. He's very astute, puts his money where his mouth is and has shared invaluable tips and information on scaling businesses through various media, both free and paid. I've been privileged to attend sessions that my own business coach invited Dan to deliver, and I must admit to being a bit of a fan girl. Look up Dan Priestley's stuff. You won't regret it.

One of the approaches that Dan has taken to growing his start-up businesses, with a great deal of success, is to mimic a method that the British Army has been using for centuries.

Scaling Like a Boss: The British Army Formula

Now, you might be wondering what the British Army has to do with your business. Well, unless you're planning a hostile takeover of your competitors (which I don't recommend), probably not much. But hear me out. Their organisational structure, refined over 400 years, offers some valuable lessons for scaling your business.

Daniel Priestley swears by this approach. Here's the gist (which we're going to look at in more depth in the next chapter):

Scout team. Two people assessing opportunities or threats. In business terms, this could be you and a trusted advisor scoping out new markets.

Fire team. Four people tackling urgent problems. Think of this as your crack team for putting out fires (hopefully not literal ones).

Section. Eight people handling day-to-day operations. This is your dream team for getting stuff done.

The key takeaway? The Army never sends someone out alone. So, stop trying to be a one-person army in your business. It's exhausting, and frankly, it's holding you back.

I'm a big fan of finding something that has worked elsewhere and replicating it rather than reinventing the wheel. Too many times have I heard fledgling business owners lament, "That won't work for my business," which is often simply untrue. Think of somebody else's strategy as a recipe. If I gave you a recipe for a simple Spaghetti Bolognese, you wouldn't say, "I can't follow that because my spatula is a different shape from yours," would you? And, like all good recipes, once you've mastered the foundation dish, it's a lot easier to embellish to your own tastes afterwards.

So, if you don't fancy the strategy Daniel Priestley uses, that's fine. But you do need a strategy. My advice is to focus on the people and skills that will facilitate growth, rather than creating more tasks and reports for you to manage. In the simplest of terms, this means prioritising the hiring of a senior leadership team and your sales peeps.

Physician Heal Thyself

One of my coaching clients is another recruitment business based in the West Midlands. The founders are great and very experienced. They help other businesses grow and provide advice on staffing and team-related issues. Yet, much like me at times, their own people strategy hasn't been properly mapped out. We have just started to draft it out, and it immediately became clear what the next hires need to be to drive the business forward. If we hadn't, they would still be taking on apprentices and trainees over experienced hires.

Will they grow the business this way? Yes.

Will it be a cheaper option than bringing in more experienced and senior hires? Yes, cheaper, but at what cost?

Will it take longer and be harder work than if they hire people who can bring skills to the table and know as much, if not more, than they do? Yes.

Will they have as much time and energy to spend on crucial elements of growing the business if they're knee-deep in training inexperienced hires or dealing with the mistakes that they will inevitably (and should be allowed to) make? No!

Are you going to grow a multi-million-pound business using trainees, apprentices or your Aunt Janet's neighbour? Unlikely, unless Auntie Janet lives next door to Richard Branson – who would probably advise you to hire strategically!

So, whatever you do for your clients and customers, whatever your passion or purpose is, make sure your strategy allows you to focus on that and your areas of genius or joy. Also, have a clear idea of who you need in place to handle all the other tasks.

Most of us are really great at coming up with solutions for other people's problems. How often have you found that the exact thing you solve for your clients is an area of improvement needed within your own business? A good strategy will help to avoid this and make sure that you take your own brilliant advice.

Leadership and Sales: Your Growth Catalysts

As you start building your team, focus on two key areas: leadership and sales. Get these right, and you'll find you have fewer plates to spin. Your stress levels will drop, you'll sleep better at night, and you'll be able to focus on growing your business instead of drowning in the day-to-day. Most importantly, you'll be on your way to achieving the time and financial freedom you crave.

Building Your Leadership Dream Team

Leadership isn't just about bossing people around (though sometimes that's fun). It's about inspiring, guiding, and empowering your team. Invest in leadership development – for yourself and your key players. Trust me, it's worth it. I've seen businesses transform when leaders learn to lead, not just manage.

Supercharging Your Sales Function

Sales are the lifeblood of your business. Get the wrong people selling, and you'll stifle your growth and send your stress levels through the roof. At worst, it could lead to your business failing. But get it right, and you'll be unstoppable.

Look for salespeople who understand that business is a team sport. They should be able to collaborate with other departments, establish long-term relationships, and prioritise the right clients. Remember, it's not just about closing deals; it's about closing the right deals.

Your People, Your Success Story

The best time to start thinking about your people strategy was when you first had the idea to start your business. The second-best time is now. Your team isn't just a workforce; they're the heart and soul of your scaling efforts. Invest in them wisely, and they'll propel your business to new heights.

Remember, you're not just building a business; you're building a team that will help you achieve your dreams. So, forget about finding unicorns and start assembling your misfit dream team. Trust me, it's a lot more fun (and effective) that way.

Now, go forth and scale! And if you need me, I'll be working on my synchronised swimming routine. You know, just in case this whole business advice thing doesn't work out.

Chapter 2
Developing a Winning Recruitment Strategy

Most business owners have a dream of what their company could become. Perhaps you're envisioning a thriving enterprise with multiple departments humming along efficiently. Or maybe you're picturing yourself finally having the freedom to focus on the parts of the business you love, rather than drowning in the day-to-day operations that drain your energy. Whatever your vision, there's one universal truth: You can't build a remarkable business alone. As the old saying goes, if you want to go fast, go alone; if you want to go far, go together.

But here's the rub: Most entrepreneurs approach hiring as a reactive scramble rather than a strategic process. They wait until they're drowning in work and desperate for help before posting a hastily written job advert. Then they wonder why they end up with mediocre talent that creates more problems than it solves.

I've seen this pattern repeat countless times, and I'm here to tell you there's a better way. A way that transforms recruitment from a necessary evil into a powerful growth engine for your business.

Why You Need a Recruitment Strategy (and Not Just a "We're Hiring!" Post)

Let's be brutally honest, randomly hiring people when you feel overwhelmed is about as strategic as trying to put out a house fire with a water pistol. It might make you feel like you're doing something, but it's woefully inadequate for the task at hand.

A proper recruitment strategy isn't just about filling seats; it's about methodically building the team that will take your business where you want it to go. It's about looking beyond your immediate needs to create a framework for sustainable growth. Without a recruitment strategy, you're essentially playing business roulette. You might get lucky occasionally, but the odds are stacked against you. And in today's competitive talent market, can you really afford to leave your company's future to chance?

Think about it this way: would you launch a new product without a marketing plan? Would you expand to a new location without financial projections? Of course not. So why would you approach building your team, arguably your most valuable asset, without a clear strategy?

A well-crafted recruitment strategy helps you:

Avoid costly hiring mistakes. The wrong hire doesn't just waste salary; they can damage team morale, customer relationships, and your brand reputation. A strategic approach dramatically reduces these risks.

Attract better talent. When you know exactly who you need and why, you can craft compelling job descriptions and employer branding that speak directly to your ideal candidates.

Build for the future, not just the present. A recruitment strategy forces you to think beyond putting out today's fires and consider what your business will need to thrive tomorrow.

Save time and money. Structured recruitment processes are more efficient, reducing the time positions remain unfilled and minimising the resources spent on finding the right people.

When we first started working with Your Doctor Film & Media (YDFM), there was no clear plan or strategy in place. The pace and volume at which their first contract was growing didn't allow for that. It was literally all hands on deck and throwing people at them. The first hires were primarily there to liaise with the client and ensure everyone's satisfaction, as well as to inform YDFM about the production company's requirements and the necessary personnel and testing protocols for COVID-19 clearance before being allowed on set. At short notice. With ever-changing schedules.

We had a very broad brief: people who could work on set and locations for long and often unsocial hours; who could think on their feet when faced with changing requirements; and who were good with people who could be demanding, relentless and used to getting what they want. Whilst riding a unicycle and juggling flaming torches! OK, so I added the last bit, but that's kind of what it felt like at the time.

Luckily, I've been doing this for a long time, and my AuDHD brain is excellent at seeing solutions that aren't always immediately obvious to the neurotypical (or Muggles, as I call them). Straight away, I thought to myself, "This sounds like people who've worked in events and hospitality for ages, and we'll get some brilliant people managers in the mix too, because everyone has been furloughed or made redundant in that sector. Win, win, win, I reckon!" I also had a feeling that this thing was going to really take off, even though none of us knew how long the lockdowns and pandemic would last, and that YDFM would need people who could step up into senior roles quickly and lead their own teams. Turns out, I was right.

The first placements included Sergiu, who had been the Events Manager for the Royal Opera House in Covent Garden for over a decade; Laura, who had been a project and events manager for companies such as Disney and Merlin Entertainment; and Sam, who was an event manager, actor and producer. They all ended up as heads of divisions and running large teams and special projects. Their ability to step up meant that the company could scale more quickly, as they could be relied upon to grow the team and get things done without the founders having to get involved in everything. This succession planning is just one aspect to consider when drafting a people plan.

As this business was born out of necessity, and we all believed the pandemic would be relatively short-lived, the whole thing was largely reactive until we reached a point where the business simply grew too big to continue in that way. In hindsight, we should have considered a strategy a bit earlier in the process. It would have allowed us to map out which roles would evolve rapidly if the company went in one direction and what would happen if it went in another. By not doing this, we ended up in a position where a couple of roles (notably an HR Manager role) should probably have been fulfilled by an interim contractor or outsourced to a consultant. The business needs had evolved fairly rapidly, shifting from a transactional and task-oriented role to a strategic and transformational one that requires different skill sets and a completely different level of expertise.

Creating Your Recruitment Masterplan: From Chaos to Clarity

So you're convinced you need a strategy (brilliant!), but where do you start? Let's break this down into manageable steps that will transform your approach to building your team. You can't go far wrong if you follow my 5-Step Recruitment Masterplan.

Step 1: Design the Business You Want, Not the One You Have

This is where Michael Gerber's E-Myth wisdom comes into play. Most business owners make the critical mistake of creating an organisational chart based on their current situation. But that's backwards thinking.

Instead, design the organisational structure for the business you want to build. Yes, I'm serious. Create an organisational chart for your ideal version of the company, even if it's just you and your cat working from your spare bedroom right now.

This exercise forces you to think strategically about every function your business needs to thrive. Marketing, operations, finance, customer service, product development – map it all out. Who reports to whom? What are the key responsibilities of each role? What skills and experience will each position require?

Don't worry about how you'll fill all these positions immediately. That's not the point. The point is to create a roadmap for growth – a clear vision of where you're heading.

Once you've created this dream org chart, you can work backwards to determine which positions need to be filled first, which can be combined temporarily and which can wait until you've reached certain growth milestones.

Step 2: Take Personal Responsibility (Even for the Roles You Haven't Filled Yet)

Here's another E-Myth gem that seems counterintuitive at first: Sign your name to every position on that org chart, even the ones you haven't hired for yet.

Why? Because until you find the right person, you're responsible for ensuring that the function is performed adequately. This creates accountability and prevents critical business functions from falling through the cracks.

It also forces you to thoroughly understand each role before hiring for it. How can you effectively recruit for a position if you don't fully grasp what success in that role looks like?

Taking personal responsibility doesn't mean you have to do everything yourself (that would defeat the purpose!). It means you need to ensure everything gets done, whether through your own efforts, outsourcing, automation, or strategic hiring.

Step 3: Adopt the British Army Approach to Team Building

This is where Daniel Priestley's brilliant adaptation of military team structure comes into play. The British Army has spent centuries perfecting the art of building effective teams, and there's much we can learn from their approach.

In this model, teams are structured around four key roles:

1. **The Leader (Commander).** This person sets the vision, makes key decisions and takes ultimate responsibility for outcomes. In your business, this might be you as the founder or CEO.

2. **The Doer (Operator).** These are your specialists who execute the core functions of your business. They have deep expertise in their areas and deliver your products or services.

3. **The Dealmaker (Intelligence).** These individuals connect your business to opportunities, clients and partners. They're outward-facing, relationship-focused and bring in business.

4. **The Systems Person (Logistics).** These detail-oriented team members create processes, track metrics, and ensure everything runs smoothly behind the scenes.

Every effective team needs all four elements. You might start by wearing multiple hats yourself, but as you grow, you'll need to fill these roles with specialists who excel in their respective areas.

The beauty of this model is its scalability. As your business grows, you can replicate this structure across departments, creating mini-teams that each have these four elements represented.

Step 4: Map Your Current Skills and Identify the Gaps

Now it's time for some honest self-assessment. Which of these roles do you naturally excel in? Where are your weaknesses?

Most entrepreneurs have strengths in one or two areas but struggle in others. Perhaps you're a brilliant Dealmaker who can charm clients and close sales, but you lack the Systems Person's attention to detail. Or maybe you're an exceptional Doer with deep technical expertise, but you're uncomfortable in the Leader role. Identifying these gaps is crucial because they represent your first strategic hires. You want to bring in people whose strengths complement your weaknesses, creating a balanced team that can tackle any challenge.

Step 5: Prioritise Your Hiring Plan

With your dream org chart in one hand and your skills assessment in the other, you can now create a prioritised hiring plan. This isn't just about filling positions; it's about strategically building capability in your business.

Ask yourself:

Which roles, if filled, would create the biggest impact on business growth?

Which functions are currently causing the most pain or limiting your ability to scale?

Which positions could generate revenue that would fund further hiring?

Remember, your first hires are absolutely critical. They'll help shape your company culture and will likely take on leadership roles as you grow. Take your time to find the right people, even if it means temporary discomfort.

The Interim Solution: When Permanent Isn't Always Perfect

Now, here's where many business owners go wrong: They assume every role needs to be filled with a permanent, full-time employee. However, in today's flexible work environment, that's no longer the case, especially for fast-growing businesses where roles evolve rapidly. Sometimes, the smartest move is to bring in interim talent or outsource certain functions before committing to a permanent hire. This approach offers several advantages:

Speed and agility. Interim professionals can be onboarded almost immediately, ensuring minimal disruption to operations. This is particularly valuable when you need specialised skills for a specific project or to fill a sudden vacancy.

Access to high-level expertise. Interim executives and specialists bring a wealth of experience from working across various industries and projects. They can hit the ground running with minimal training. There will be times when they tell you what to do. Surround yourself with people who know more than you and learn from them. Better still, get out of their way and let them do their magic while you hocus focus on yours!

Cost-effectiveness. For roles that are still evolving or for specialised functions that don't require full-time attention, interim or outsourced solutions can be more economical than permanent hires. If an experienced expert can sort your issue, complete your project, and implement your system in three or six months, why would you hire somebody at that level for years on end, when a more modest salary level could keep on top of it once the tricky stuff is sorted?

Flexibility. As your business grows and evolves, your needs will also change. Interim arrangements give you the flexibility to adapt without the complications of restructuring a permanent team.

Try before you buy. Working with someone on an interim basis provides an opportunity to assess their skills and cultural fit before considering them for a permanent position.

This approach is particularly valuable in fast-growth environments where roles and requirements can change rapidly. Perhaps you need a CFO's expertise but can't justify a full-time salary yet. Or maybe you need specialised marketing help to launch a new product, but won't require that specific skill set long-term.

Recruitment Process Outsourcing (RPO) is another option worth considering, especially if you're planning significant growth. RPO providers can manage your entire recruitment process, from sourcing to onboarding, allowing you to scale your hiring efforts efficiently without the need to build a large internal HR team. It's one of the solutions we offer to clients who would benefit from that approach.

Putting It All Together: Your Recruitment Strategy in Action

So you've designed your dream org chart, identified your skill gaps, prioritised your hiring needs, and considered flexible staffing options. Now it's time to put it all together into a cohesive recruitment strategy. Your strategy should include:

Clear job descriptions for each role. These should outline not just responsibilities and requirements, but also how the position contributes to your company's mission and growth.

Your employer brand messaging. What makes your company a great place to work? Why should talented people choose you over competitors? Your recruitment strategy should articulate your unique value proposition as an employer.

Sourcing channels. Where will you find your ideal candidates? This might include job boards, social media, professional networks, referral programs or recruitment partners. Remember that your ideal candidate may not be actively seeking a new role but may consider a move for the right role. These people are not looking at job boards and hiring adverts. This is where somebody like me, an experienced search specialist, will come into their own. Recent estimates indicate that approximately 15% of the workforce is seeking a new job at any given time. And around 30% will not move regardless of what's on offer. That means that 55% of the people you want to talk to must be found, and a well-crafted outreach conversation must be initiated. That takes significant time and resources. This is why successful businesses use a professional recruiter or search specialist (AKA a headhunter) to make that happen. And it doesn't have to be for only senior hires, either.

Selection process. How will you assess candidates? Will you use interviews, skills tests, trial projects or other evaluation methods? Your process should be thorough but efficient.

Onboarding plan. How will you integrate new team members and ensure they are set up for success? A structured onboarding process reduces time-to-productivity and improves retention.

Budget and timeline. What resources will you allocate to recruitment, and what is your hiring timeline? Being realistic about both is essential for successful implementation.

Remember, your recruitment strategy isn't set in stone. It should be a living document that evolves as your business grows and market conditions change. Review and refine it regularly to ensure it continues to serve your business goals.

The Unicorn Myth: Building Your Team of Brilliant Misfits

Let's end with a reality check. The perfect candidate doesn't exist. Just like unicorns with rainbow manes and glittery farts, the mythical hire who ticks every box on your wish-list is a fantasy. What you're really looking for is a team of brilliant misfits. People whose unique combinations of strengths, weaknesses, and quirks come together to create something greater than the sum of its parts. The most successful businesses aren't built by perfect individuals; they're built by complementary teams who share a vision and bring different perspectives and skills to the table. So stop chasing unicorns and start building your band of brilliant misfits. With a strategic approach to recruitment, you'll find the right people to help you turn your business dreams into reality. And remember, the best time to create your recruitment strategy was when you first started your business. The second-best time is now.

And if you've just read this and thought, "Holy shit, I don't know where to start with all this!", you can find some free resources on my website www.recruitrecruit.co.uk/freeresources or call to find out how we can help you with it.

Chapter 3
From 0 to £30 Million Turnover in 21 Months: A Case Study

The global COVID pandemic was a tumultuous time that brought death, devastation, economic uncertainty, mental health issues, and many opportunities for reflection and finding solutions. It wasn't just fans of Friends who were shouting "PIVOT!" and discovering new ways of working.

One of those new opportunities presented itself to a doctor in Buckinghamshire, who said yes to the unknown, ended up founding a new business that grew rapidly and exponentially, and required lots of lovely, experienced people to make it happen.

Before we examine the journey that led them to thirty million in turnover in such a short amount of time, we need to consider what could be holding you back from achieving the same success. The first thing to ask is, "Am I saying yes to opportunities?" And, if not, what's holding you back? You might be worried that you don't have the funds to grow at the moment. You might have had a bad experience previously. Did you take on somebody who didn't work out? Do you think that you don't want the hassle of managing people? Do you think you don't have the time to train somebody whom you take on?

I could make lists all day. Whatever the reason or excuse for putting off your growth or starting to employ people, it generally boils down to fear. A fear of something. Fear can paralyse us. But, you know what, it's scary trying something, and it's just as scary sitting back and doing nothing…or just doing what we've always done.

So, now that we've recognised we need to embrace that fear and just get on with things, let's have a look at what can happen when you do just that.

Here's how I like to describe it in a mini brochure we send out (more sporadically, and nowhere near as much as we should!):

We were first approached to help Your Doctor Film & Media in May 2020.

They had been engaged to deliver COVID-19 testing services and protocols, allowing filming to continue on *Jurassic World: Dominion* at Pinewood Studios. It was the first major production movie to resume filming during the pandemic. Word soon got out, much like the T. rex in the Jurassic World films, and all hell broke loose, with media and film companies clamouring for their services. With only a handful of staff at the time, it was clear that they needed a lot of people QUICKLY.

Like a herd of weirdly cute and deceptively fast Velociraptors, we sprang into action and chased all the talent, kicking and screaming with delight, into their arms. And they all lived happily ever after. The end.

The category spread was vast and included administrators, finance, HR, CEOs, sales and business development, IT and developers, analysts, biomedical scientists, laboratory technicians, department heads, nurses and clinicians, client relationship managers, trainers, and a variety of contractors.

Of course, that makes it sound much easier than it actually was.

I'm a big-picture thinker, so that would be enough to sell me on it if I were looking to scale in scope and pace. And I know that many of you will want to know more about the why and how, so you can either replicate it yourself or make an informed decision about who and how you will outsource this business-critical growth function to.

So, what really happened, and how did we get involved?

The doctor, Riccardo Di Cuffa, is the brother of a good friend of mine and has a couple of private clinics. One of them is not very far from the world-famous Pinewood Studios. Someone from the production company, Arkadian, approached Ric to see if he could conduct COVID-19 tests to keep the talent safe and adhere to the appropriate protocols in place to prevent the unchecked spread of the virus. It turns out that the film they were working on was *Jurassic World: Dominion,* which was one of the first major movies to resume production during the lockdown periods. We were all stuck at home, binge-watching films and TV shows, discovering arts and crafts and new hobbies. And Your Doctor Film & Media (YDFM) was born and played its part in ensuring that production houses could continue creating content for us to consume.

The Early Days: Reactive Recruitment

The initial months were a whirlwind of activity, marked by a sense of urgency and rapid adaptation. The demand for COVID-19 testing services surged unexpectedly, leaving us scrambling to keep up with the pace. It was a period of pure pandemonium, with our focus squarely on recruiting people as quickly as possible to meet the escalating needs of our client.

During this chaotic period, we found ourselves drawing heavily from the hospitality and events sectors. Many individuals from these industries had been furloughed or made redundant due to the pandemic, and they possessed the exact attributes we needed. They were accustomed to working long and anti-social hours, had the ability to think on their feet, and were skilled at interacting with people of all dispositions and levels of seniority. These traits made them ideal candidates for the fast-paced environment.

As we navigated this reactive phase, we were fortunate to tap into a pool of talented individuals who were eager to transition into new roles. Their adaptability and resilience were invaluable assets as we worked tirelessly to meet the growing demand. However, it soon became apparent that this approach, while effective in the short term, needed to evolve into a more strategic and sustainable model.

Transitioning to a Strategic Approach

After the initial triage phase, we all recognised the need for a more deliberate and forward-thinking approach to recruitment and talent management. It was at this juncture that Vanessa Di Cuffa, the aforementioned sister of Dr. Ric, and a dual-qualified Employment Lawyer and HR Specialist, played a pivotal role in transforming the strategy. With her extensive experience in HR and employment law, she brought a depth of knowledge that was instrumental in planning and profiling support functions and leaders within the business.

Vanessa's expertise allowed us to refine our recruitment processes, focusing on identifying and attracting candidates who not only possessed the necessary skills but also aligned with the organisational culture and values. Her work involved creating detailed profiles for key roles, ensuring that we were targeting individuals who could drive growth and innovation within YDFM. This strategic shift marked a significant turning point, enabling us to build a more robust and resilient team capable of meeting both current and future challenges.

Collaboration with Independent Recruiters

As we continued to evolve and refine our recruitment strategy, we recognised the importance of collaboration with trusted independent recruiters. By partnering with these experts, we were able to adopt an agile model that allowed us to react quickly to changing circumstances and anticipate future talent needs. This partnership allowed us to access a wide range of sector-specific skills and categories, ensuring that we could adapt to any shift in market demands.

In a time when many solo recruiters were struggling to keep their businesses going, it also meant that we could support other small businesses, and I could work with people I'd grown to know, like and trust over the years in the recruitment industry.

The agility provided by these collaborations was invaluable. It enabled us to pivot rapidly in response to emerging trends and talent shortages, ensuring that we remained competitive in a rapidly changing landscape. Moreover, working with other independent recruiters provided us with access to a broader talent pool, allowing us to identify and attract top candidates who might have otherwise been overlooked.

This collaborative approach also facilitated a more proactive stance on talent acquisition. Rather than merely reacting to immediate needs, we were able to anticipate and prepare for future skill requirements. This forward-thinking mindset allowed us to build a diverse and dynamic workforce, equipped to drive innovation and growth across the organisation.

Building for the Future

As I look back on this journey, it's clear that our ability to adapt and evolve has been crucial to our success. From the initial reactive phase to the more strategic approach that followed, each step contributed to building a robust and scalable business. The collaboration with independent recruiters was a key factor in this process, allowing us to stay agile and responsive to changing market conditions.

Moving forward, we recognise that the talent landscape will continue to evolve, influenced by factors such as technological advancements and shifting workforce dynamics. Our strategic partnerships and agile recruitment model position us well to navigate these changes, ensuring that we remain at the forefront of innovation and talent acquisition.

In conclusion, this journey taught me the importance of flexibility, strategic planning and collaboration in scaling at pace. As we continue to grow and evolve, we remain committed to maintaining a proactive and adaptive approach to talent management, continually seeking new ways to attract, retain and develop the best talent available for any client that works with us.

Reflections and Lessons Learned

Reflecting on these experiences, several key lessons stand out:

Adaptability is key. The ability to adapt quickly to changing circumstances has been crucial. Whether it's responding to surging demand or shifting market trends, flexibility is essential for survival and success.

Strategic planning. Moving from a reactive to a strategic approach has allowed us to build a more sustainable and resilient organisation. This involves not just recruiting for immediate needs but also planning for future talent requirements.

Collaboration and partnerships. Working with independent recruiters has provided us with the agility and access to a broader talent pool. This partnership has been instrumental in helping us stay competitive and responsive to market changes.

Cultural alignment. Ensuring that new recruits align with organisational culture and values has been vital. This not only enhances team cohesion but also drives long-term success and retention.

Continuous learning. The ever-changing talent landscape means that continuous learning and innovation are essential. Staying abreast of the latest trends and technologies in recruitment will remain a priority as we move forward.

By embracing these lessons and continuing to evolve our approach, we are confident in our ability to navigate future challenges and opportunities, ensuring that we remain a leader in our field and that founders and CEOs who want to scale at pace or build towards an exit can partner with us in confidence.

Looking to the Future

As we move forward, several trends and challenges will shape our approach to talent management, and one of the biggest is currently digital transformation. The increasing use of technology in recruitment will continue to transform how we identify, attract, and retain talent. Leveraging digital tools and platforms will be crucial for accessing a wider pool of candidates and streamlining our recruitment processes. There are already hundreds of new platforms and providers out there, and they are growing every day. To ensure continued and sustainable growth in your business, it will be a project in itself to stay on top of the digital tools that will help you find and connect with the talent you need.

Remote work is another hot topic and has grown largely as a result of the global pandemic. The rise of remote work presents both opportunities and challenges. It allows us to access talent from a broader geographic area, but also requires us to adapt our management and communication strategies to ensure that remote workers feel connected and valued. It can be really convenient, and numerous studies have shown that productivity increases in most cases. However, we have to make sure that everybody has very clear objectives and that the culture, vision, and purpose of your business are understood and shared by everyone on the team.

Sustainability and culture have become increasingly important in modern businesses as our understanding of their benefits has grown. As individuals and organisations become increasingly focused on sustainability and social responsibility, these factors will play a larger role in attracting and retaining talent. Ensuring that our organisational culture aligns with these values will be essential for attracting like-minded individuals. As a recruiter with nearly thirty years of experience, I have witnessed a significant shift in the importance of purpose and the social value a business brings when candidates are considering a move. It's also something that many clients now look for from their suppliers. Is your business sustainable? And how will your recruiting strategies ensure that you are? What does your succession planning look like? Have you even thought about it?

Agility and adaptability have always been key factors in the success and survival of businesses. Survival of the fittest has always been about who is best equipped to adapt to change. The ability to adapt quickly to changing market conditions will remain critical. This involves not just responding to immediate needs but also anticipating future trends and talent shortages. I'm sure that we can all agree that we've seen bigger, quicker, and more incredible changes in how businesses are run, market themselves, and deliver results in the past decade than we've seen in the previous century.

By focusing on these areas and continually refining our approach, we are well-positioned to meet the challenges of the future and continue to grow and thrive as an organisation.

This journey with YDFM was marked by challenge and opportunity, which contributed to the growth and resilience of both businesses. From the early days of reactive recruitment to the strategic partnerships that now underpin our talent management strategy and agile model, every step has been crucial.

In the end, it's clear that the path forward will require ongoing evolution and adaptation. However, with a strong foundation built on strategic planning, collaboration, and a commitment to cultural alignment, I am confident in our ability to help clients navigate the complexities of the modern talent landscape and emerge stronger and more resilient than ever.

Chapter 4
Do I Need a Professional Recruiter?

We've examined how a lack of time is one of the major factors affecting an entrepreneur's ability to hire effectively. If you need to hire because you're being pulled from pillar to post, or cannot physically grow the business anymore because you're at full capacity (or breaking point could be closer to the truth), then it stands to reason that adding a comprehensive and robust search and recruitment campaign and process to your to-do list is a terrible idea. Even if you're really experienced and good at hiring people, you simply won't have the time to give it your full attention. And, if you're not focusing totally on the people you're bringing into your business, then costly hiring mistakes will be made. And by "costly," I mean financially, time-wise and, most importantly, to your mental health and sanity.

If you are giving your undivided attention to the recruitment process, which can take weeks or even months, then what is being overlooked in your business?

Many people attempt to do it themselves because they believe recruitment fees are too expensive. But in comparison to what? Most founders and entrepreneurs who try to do it all themselves rarely factor in the cost of their time, the cost of what doesn't get done while they're focusing on hiring, and the cost of getting it wrong. This happens all too often when people lack experience in interviewing and hiring, don't have a clear people strategy and are distracted by a million other things to do. Remember that many large organisations don't use recruitment agencies because they can afford the fees. They use them because they've done the time and motion studies, which show how the investment in a good recruiter is cost-effective.

This is why the most successful people outsource the problem to the experts. There are some businesses that do all of their recruitment in-house and to great effect. So, how do you decide whether you need to bring in the professionals or not?

Just ask yourself some simple questions:

Is there somebody in the business who can dedicate all their time and attention to growing the teams for several months?

Does that person have experience and a good track record in talent acquisition, interviewing, and selection?

Do you have a workable people strategy in place?

Do you have the time and money available to start from scratch if/when a hire goes wrong?

Will you still achieve your goals if you fail to get the right people in place at the right time?

If the answer to one or more of these questions is no, then you should seriously consider using a professional recruiter.

When you're looking to scale your business rapidly, the margin for error in hiring becomes razor-thin. Every new hire must be a strategic addition, capable of driving your business forward rather than holding it back. This is precisely why turning to a professional recruiter isn't just a convenience; it's a strategic imperative.

Over the years, I've met with many small business owners and founders who have created a great deal of stress and financial loss for themselves by making an early hiring mistake. This is often because they tend to "go with their gut" or hire people who are incredibly similar to them. While this means you'll probably get on well with your new hire and feel like you understand each other and communicate well, being too similar can also create its own set of problems. At best, you will likely have similar strengths and areas that you both aren't so hot on. And you will both work best with clients or customers who have certain personality traits and behavioural styles. This can be really limiting in a business. Especially one that is looking to scale. All the talk about diversity in businesses and organisations is more than a purely ethical and moral obligation. It has been high on the agenda for those who are serious about growth and improvement for the past few years, as diversity in the workforce has been shown to enhance performance and profitability. At worst, your similarities can lead to resentment and arguments. It's a simple fact of life that the people who tend to annoy and irritate us more than anyone else are often those who are the most similar. We subconsciously spot the behaviours and reactions that we don't really like in ourselves, and it winds us up no end. We've all heard somebody say something like, "You and your mum don't get along because you're so alike!"

Having an external party assess your recruitment and team in a more detached and dispassionate manner can be highly beneficial in ensuring you find someone with whom you can work well, while capitalising on each other's different fields of expertise and strengths. Here are some other reasons why the right professional will add more value than doing it yourself:

Access to a Larger, More Qualified Talent Pool

One of the most significant advantages professional recruiters bring is their extensive network and access to a much broader talent pool than you could ever reach on your own. While your job postings might attract active job seekers, recruiters tap into hidden networks of passive candidates. Those highly skilled professionals who aren't actively searching but are open to the right opportunity. These passive candidates often represent the highest-quality talent available, and without a recruiter's extensive network and proactive approach, they would remain entirely invisible to your hiring efforts.

Expertise in Candidate Evaluation

The process of screening and vetting candidates is not only time-consuming but also requires specific expertise. Professional recruiters are trained to assess not just technical skills but also cultural fit and long-term potential within your organisation. They know how to ask the right questions, probe beneath surface-level answers, and evaluate candidates' true capabilities through structured interviews and assessments. This meticulous approach significantly reduces the risk of costly hiring mistakes that can set your business back months or even years.

Speed and Efficiency

When scaling at pace, speed matters. A vacant position doesn't just mean lost productivity. It means added stress on existing teams, delayed projects and potentially missed growth opportunities. Professional recruiters streamline every stage of the hiring process, from crafting compelling job descriptions and managing job postings across multiple platforms to conducting initial interviews and shortlisting only the strongest candidates. With their established processes and dedicated resources, recruiters can fill roles significantly faster than most businesses can manage internally. In fact, recruitment agencies typically reduce time-to-hire by weeks compared to in-house efforts.

Cost-Effectiveness

It's understandable that businesses worry about recruitment fees. But consider this: What is the true cost of handling recruitment yourself? When you factor in your own time spent away from core business activities, plus the hidden costs associated with advertising roles, screening applicants, interviewing candidates, negotiating salaries, onboarding new hires (and repeating the entire process if a hire doesn't work out), the financial implications quickly spiral out of control. Studies show that outsourcing recruitment can reduce hiring costs by 30% to 50% compared to managing it internally. Moreover, recruiters have deep market knowledge that enables them to negotiate competitive salaries effectively, saving you money while ensuring you attract top talent.

Enhanced Employer Branding

In today's competitive talent market, your employer brand matters more than ever. Professional recruiters don't just find candidates; they actively promote your company as an attractive place to work. They craft compelling job descriptions that resonate with ideal candidates by clearly communicating their company's culture, values and unique selling points. They also maintain consistent communication with applicants throughout the recruitment process, ensuring a positive candidate experience that enhances your reputation as an employer of choice.

Long-Term Talent Strategy

Professional recruiters don't merely fill vacancies; they help build sustainable talent pipelines for future growth. They identify potential candidates who might not be ready now but could be ideal for future roles or leadership positions. This proactive approach ensures you're never scrambling when critical positions become vacant. Additionally, recruiters assist with succession planning by grooming internal talent for future leadership roles, ensuring continuity and stability as your business expands.

Reduced Administrative Burden

Recruitment involves significant administrative effort. From managing job postings across multiple platforms to handling extensive paperwork and compliance checks. Outsourcing these administrative tasks frees up valuable internal resources, allowing you to focus on strategic objectives and day-to-day operations. The result? Your team remains focused on driving growth rather than being bogged down in administrative tasks.

Improved Candidate Experience

A professional recruiter maintains consistent communication with candidates throughout the hiring process. This creates a positive candidate experience that reflects well on your company, even for those who don't ultimately get hired. A good candidate experience enhances your reputation in the market and ensures top talent remains interested in future opportunities with your business.

Avoidance of Common Hiring Pitfalls

Hiring mistakes are costly. Financially, strategically and culturally. Common pitfalls include rushing through the selection process due to urgency, overlooking cultural alignment, setting unclear role expectations or failing to assess real-world skills beyond an interview performance adequately. Professional recruiters employ structured processes and proven methodologies specifically designed to avoid these pitfalls.

Scalability

Perhaps most importantly for businesses looking to scale quickly, professional recruiters offer scalability in their services. Whether you need one key hire or fifty new team members within months, recruitment agencies have the resources and infrastructure already in place to handle volume hiring efficiently. Their flexible model means you pay only for what you need, when you need it, without committing long-term resources internally.

The Power of a Professional Recruiter

When Your Doctor Film & Media was created to provide the COVID-19 testing protocols required for *Jurassic World Dominion* to resume production, the then-unknown nature of the pandemic (and our response of staying at home and consuming more entertainment media than ever) meant that they were destined to be successful. There were few competitors in the market as the service had never been needed before. Unsurprisingly, it exploded pretty quickly.

Founder Dr. Riccardo Di Cuffa may well have tried to recruit the people he needed as demands grew. And he managed to secure some really pivotal people early on. Peter Watts, his co-founder and CEO, and Vanessa Di Cuffa, his sister and a real heavy hitter as a Chief People Officer. Vanessa consulted with the business and advised them that I get involved early on. Luckily, Pete has grown other businesses and appreciates the efficiencies in getting the experts in early. So, while the success of the business is their doing, they wouldn't have had the capacity (time or mental) to focus on their areas of genius if they were caught up in recruiting the rapidly growing teams that were needed. Pete kindly provided a testimonial (which you will have seen in the introduction to this book) and stated that they "couldn't have done it without us." They could have continued to service the original contract with the first production company, Arkadian, but they couldn't have kept up with that and had the time to find the people who would enable them to secure new contracts and deliver on those contracts as well. You can grow your business significantly without a professional recruiter, but will you do it as quickly or as well?

Long-Term Strategic Partnership

Finally, it's worth noting that professional recruiters strive to establish long-term relationships with their clients. They invest time understanding your company's culture, values, goals and strategic direction, ensuring they're always aligned with your vision when sourcing candidates. Over time, this partnership becomes increasingly valuable as they learn exactly what makes someone successful within your unique environment.

In conclusion, attempting DIY recruitment when scaling rapidly is often penny-wise but pound-foolish. The hidden costs, in terms of lost productivity due to diverted attention from core business activities, missed opportunities due to slow hiring, potential damage from poor candidate experiences and increased turnover from unsuitable hires, all add up quickly.

By partnering with a professional recruiter instead, you:

- Gain access immediately to a wider pool of high-quality talent
- Leverage expert knowledge about market conditions
- Save significant amounts of time (and therefore money)
- Improve both short-term efficiency (faster hires) and long-term effectiveness (better retention rates)

Ultimately, using a professional recruiter isn't just an expense; it's an investment into building stronger teams faster so that nothing stands between you and achieving ambitious growth goals at pace.

So, now you've decided you need a professional recruiter, let's take a look at how to find the best fit for you.

Chapter 5
How Do I Choose the Right Recruiter for Me?

Choosing the right recruiter isn't a one-size-fits-all decision. Throughout my experience, I've consistently found that independent recruiters with a proven track record in working with start-ups and scale-ups typically deliver the best results. These independent recruiters bring deep sector-specific knowledge, extensive networks and a level of personalisation, agility and transparency that larger agencies often struggle to match.

But before deciding on the recruiter for you, you will need to think about what's going on in your world and what challenges you are facing in your business. Why are you thinking about recruiting now?

Are you overwhelmed, close to burnout or too busy to remember your own name? Have you secured some funding or investment and know the time is right to build your business? Do you have a mentor or business coach urging you to grow and advising you to build a team? Or do you already have a small team, and they're causing you more work rather than less? Is your growth stuck?

For most of us, the answer to the biggest blocks in our business is to get advice from an expert. Sometimes, it's right to seek advice from a mentor or consultant. Sometimes, it's right to outsource the problem. Sometimes, especially for the sake of long-term and sustainable growth, it's right to employ those experts directly.

When the time is right, it's time to find the right recruiter.

Independent recruiters genuinely understand the unique challenges faced by start-ups and scale-ups because they're entrepreneurs themselves. They appreciate ambitious growth targets, tight budgets and the critical importance of each new hire. This entrepreneurial empathy positions them as true strategic partners rather than mere order-takers.

However, beyond credentials and expertise, choosing the right recruiter often boils down to something more intangible yet equally critical: personal chemistry. Recruitment fundamentally revolves around people – understanding their motivations, values and cultural fit within your organisation. If there's a mismatch in style or values between you and your recruiter, it can lead to miscommunication, frustration and, ultimately, poor hiring decisions.

For instance, I know I'm not everyone's cup of tea, and that's perfectly fine. On the other hand, I only want to work with clients who approach our partnership at eye level. I value relationships built on mutual respect, constructive challenges to each other's thinking and a passion or purpose that always outweighs ego. If you're looking for someone who simply nods along without challenging your assumptions or pushing you to think differently about your hiring strategy, then I'm probably not the right fit for you. And that's okay.

Ultimately, selecting the right recruiter means finding someone who can become a trusted partner in your business's growth journey. Independent recruiters with proven track records supporting start-ups and scale-ups are often best positioned to deliver this partnership effectively. Their independence ensures they have skin in the game. Their reputation depends entirely on delivering excellent results for their clients. When you find an independent recruiter whose style aligns with yours and who demonstrates a genuine passion for strategically building your team, you've found a powerful ally who can help drive your business forward.

Understanding the Recruitment Industry's Reputation

Let's be honest: Recruitment doesn't have the best reputation historically. Years ago, I recall seeing recruiters ranked alongside bankers, estate agents and dodgy car salespeople on a list of least trusted professions. Some of this reputation is warranted. There are recruiters out there who are simply not skilled at their jobs or are solely driven by profit. Other aspects of this reputation are outdated hangovers from aggressive sales tactics prevalent in the 1980s and 1990s. Tactics that are now broadly rejected by an industry increasingly defined by integrity, honesty, professionalism, and improved standards.

Today's recruitment industry is fiercely competitive, driving significant improvements in training quality and service standards across the board. Yet this competition can also make choosing the right recruiter challenging once you realise you're better off focusing on growing your business while someone else handles talent acquisition.

Common Approaches Businesses Take

In my experience working with ambitious businesses, ranging from funded ventures scaling rapidly within defined timelines to solo entrepreneurs hiring their first teammates, I've observed three common approaches (often used individually or in combination):

1. Going to big brand recruitment agencies that cover multiple categories.

2. Using specialists for each hiring category (e.g., sales, finance, executive search).

3. Engaging several local or national agencies simultaneously for a wider reach.

Let's explore each option's advantages and disadvantages clearly:

Big Brand Generalist Agencies

Advantages

Big brand generalist agencies usually have extensive branch networks offering strong geographical coverage. Their familiar brands provide comfort similar to choosing Heinz baked beans or ketchup over lesser-known alternatives. Even if Aldi or Lidl have taught us that lesser-known brands can be just as good or better!

Busy founders or CEOs may find their "one-stop shop" appeal convenient. These agencies typically negotiate discounted terms for volume recruitment campaigns and exclusivity arrangements, and can excel at filling large volumes of homogeneous roles, such as call centre operatives or sales teams.

Disadvantages

- You're rarely their most important client; attention inevitably shifts toward key accounts.
- Despite their title "Recruitment Consultant," these agencies rarely consult strategically. They simply

fill orders without questioning job descriptions or aligning hires with broader business goals.

- Recruiters often lack experience in growing businesses or developing effective strategies. They merely fill orders without challenging assumptions or ensuring hires align strategically.
- They operate under strict KPIs (key performance indicators), prioritising sales calls when numbers dip. Even if it detracts from serving existing clients effectively.
- You'll likely deal with different individuals across categories unless your contract is large enough for a dedicated account manager (who won't handle day-to-day recruiting tasks).
- Their hierarchical structure limits flexibility for non-standard requests, which are common in fast-paced start-ups. Like innovative marketing tactics or non-standard pricing agreements.
- They often lack expertise in executing robust search processes for senior roles, despite enthusiastically accepting them due to the higher commissions attached.
- Corporate culture may prevent them from asking difficult questions or making challenging decisions in a constructive manner. This is something successful business leaders typically welcome.

Using Sector Specialists for Each Hiring Category

Advantages

Specialist recruiters operate within tight niches and possess strong networks relevant to your requirements. They access passive candidates who are not actively job-hunting through traditional advertisements and provide valuable market intelligence on evolving roles, salary expectations, industry trends, and candidate motivations. This information is crucial for shaping effective recruitment strategies.

Independent specialists typically offer greater personal attention, as their reputation directly impacts their livelihood.

Disadvantages

- Specialists often command higher fees (though this isn't necessarily negative if they deliver value).
- Operating within silos can lead to overlooking team dynamics when assembling teams simultaneously. Potentially resulting in mismatched behavioural styles or overly homogenous groups lacking diverse perspectives.
- Being overly focused on niche expertise might cause rigid preconceptions about suitable candidates. Potentially excluding valuable "wild card" candidates who could thrive unexpectedly.

Using Multiple Agencies Simultaneously

At first glance, engaging several agencies simultaneously might seem logical. More recruiters mean more candidates and better choices. However, unless you're hiring large volumes of temporary homogenous roles (like warehouse operatives), this is arguably one of the worst approaches you could take.

When candidates see a role advertised everywhere by multiple agencies simultaneously, they instinctively wonder what's wrong with it. Just as multiple "For Sale" signs on a house raise suspicion rather than excitement.

This approach also incurs additional administrative burdens, including managing duplicate submissions from multiple suppliers, processing numerous invoices, handling inconsistent standards and communicating with various contacts. All inefficient uses of valuable time.

Contrary to popular belief that competition among multiple agencies drives better performance, it actually creates a race-to-the-bottom mentality where speed trumps quality. Recruiters rush candidate submissions without thorough vetting (sometimes even submitting placeholder CVs without candidate consent), undermining robust selection criteria.

Are They Your Cup of Tea?

I think it's always a good idea to arrange a meeting with prospective suppliers at a very early stage. Why bugger about with quotes and proposals and information before you know whether you'd feel comfortable, or even enjoy, working with somebody? This is especially important if you're looking to scale significantly, as you will spend a lot of time talking to each other, and you need to know they get your vibe!

Once you've got a shortlist of potential suppliers, meet with all of them before deciding who to work with. Make sure that you base your decision on experience, competency and personality fit. We can be an endearing and charming bunch at times. Online meetings will suffice, but you'll get a lot more out of a lunch or dinner date. Especially if they foot the bill.

Recommendations are always a good place to start, and I've already made a case for choosing an independent operator who has earned their stripes over the big chains. Questions that I would be asking would include:

> What experience do you have working with start-ups or scale-ups?
>
> Do you collaborate with other specialists in your field?
>
> What other experts can you bring to the table to support growth phases?

What are the traits you look for in a candidate about to join a rapidly scaling, or start-up, business?

An experienced, professional recruiter will be able to find you people. Not all of them will have experience in strategy and helping you decide what and who you need in the first place. A rapidly scaling business, one undergoing transformational change or one preparing for an exit, demands a specific type of mindset and attitude. You can find somebody with the skills and experience you need, but if they don't perform well (or have a sadistic bent for) working in a rapidly changing and pivoting environment, then it's not going to end well.

Most recruiters would rather cut their own arms off than collaborate with a competitor or share the spoils. I found that the best results and a very agile way of working (as required in a fast-growing start-up or similar) are delivered by working with a variety of experts in their field and splitting the investment fairly. Pace is required, and a niche recruiter will be able to reach their established network much more quickly than a process that requires advertising and sourcing from scratch. I always say that I'm not precious about holding on to all the business, but I am precious about my clients getting the best people in place. Even if that means sharing the business with somebody else.

Business growth will often occur in sprints and spurts. A rapidly scaling business will find that the level of HR or finance support they needed six months ago is very different to what they need now. Or what they will potentially need in twelve or eighteen months' time. Working with a recruiter who has a great network of partners that can take on interim projects and inject expertise without permanently increasing headcount can be highly valuable. In fact, I was introduced to our client, which scaled to thirty million in turnover in twenty-one months, because "Bish knows everyone, and it will be really useful."

Final Thoughts

Ultimately, selecting the right recruiter involves balancing practical considerations (such as expertise and cost) against essential intangible factors like personal chemistry and alignment of values. Independent recruiters experienced in supporting start-ups often provide superior agility, personalisation, strategic insight and, crucially, genuine partnership rooted in mutual respect.

When choosing your recruiter partner:

- Prioritise genuine personal chemistry ("vibe")
- Ensure alignment on values such as transparency over profit-driven motives
- Look for strategic partnership potential rather than mere transactional relationships

- Seek recruiters willing to challenge assumptions constructively rather than simply filling orders unquestioningly

By thoughtfully considering these factors alongside the practical considerations outlined above, and avoiding pitfalls such as engaging multiple agencies simultaneously, you'll position yourself optimally for successful hires that truly drive your business forward strategically, rather than just filling vacancies reactively.

And, if you really get it right, you'll end up with a valuable mentor for your business and a sounding board. Especially if the person you end up working with is an entrepreneur and has built a business in their own right. They'll understand your challenges and provide support in areas beyond recruitment and team growth. You may even end up with a new friend!

If you read this book and think, "I'd love Bish to be my new business friend", you can contact me at sarah@recruitrecruit.co.uk to arrange a chat. Or, you can seek out additional free resources at www.recruitrecruit.co.uk.

Chapter 6
How to Get the Best Out of Your Recruiter

Let's be honest, most business relationships with recruiters are about as deep as a puddle in the Sahara. You call them when you're desperate, they send you a bunch of CVs that may or may not be relevant, you pay them an eye-watering fee, and then you both move on until the next crisis hits. It's transactional, it's shallow, and, quite frankly, it's a rubbish way to build your team.

I've spent nearly three decades in the recruitment industry, and I can tell you with absolute certainty that this approach is costing you money, time and probably your sanity too. The best recruiters aren't just CV-slinging mercenaries; they're extensions of your business, strategic partners who are as invested in your success as you are.

But here's the thing, getting the best out of your recruiter isn't just about finding someone good (though that's certainly part of it). It's about structuring the relationship in a way that sets everyone up for success. It's about understanding your role in the process and taking ownership of it. And it's about finding someone who genuinely gives a damn about your business beyond the commission cheque.

Why "Embedding" Beats "Partnership" Every Single Time

Let's start by killing a sacred cow, shall we? The word "partnership" in business has become about as meaningful as a politician's promise. Everyone claims to want a partnership with their clients, but what does that actually mean in practice?

Not much, usually.

True partnerships require equality, mutual benefit and shared risk. But the traditional recruiter-client relationship offers none of these things. The recruiter takes minimal risk, the client shoulders most of the consequences of a bad hire and the power dynamic is inherently unbalanced. Or so it seems from your point of view. On the flip side, weeks' worth of work, advertising costs, and overheads all go down the drain if a recruiter has to rebate the fee for a hire gone sideways.

What you need instead is something deeper. You need your recruiter embedded into your team unless you have your own talent acquisition team. And, even then, it can be a good idea.

Embedding means your recruiter becomes a de facto member of your organisation. They attend your team meetings. They understand your inside jokes. They know who makes the best coffee and who to avoid before 10 am. They celebrate your wins and commiserate with your losses. They're in the trenches with you, not watching from a comfortable distance.When a recruiter is embedded in your team, magical things happen:

They develop a sixth sense for cultural fit. No more candidates who look great on paper but clash horribly with your team dynamic. An embedded recruiter can tell within minutes whether someone will mesh with your quirky marketing director or your detail-obsessed operations manager.

They become proactive, not reactive. Instead of waiting for you to raise a vacancy, they're constantly scanning the horizon for talent that might benefit your business, even for positions you haven't created yet.

They represent your brand authentically. When speaking to candidates, they don't recite a generic script about your company. They speak with genuine enthusiasm and insider knowledge that no external partner could ever match.

When I worked with Your Doctor Film & Media (YDFM), I made sure that we got on-site straight away to see exactly where people would be working. Initially, this was just at Pinewood Studios, and it was an eye-opener to see how things functioned on a busy film lot. We immediately changed our approach from discussing the good salaries and the glamour of being involved in the film industry to talking about the challenges and the dynamic nature of the roles. The uncertainty and the sometimes seemingly unreasonable demands that must be satisfied. The knowledge that you could trash a million-dollar contract if you upset the wrong person. The fact that a film studio is a bit like a giant industrial site and working in a marquee and temporary offices in all weathers wasn't going to be pleasant. We discussed the possibility that your quiet Wednesday morning could suddenly erupt into panic and chaos because someone had changed the schedule for a crowd scene, and you now had to find, contact and get three hundred people in to be swabbed within the next few hours. We discussed how you would hang up after the final call, satisfied with a job well done, and then realise you were a hundred swab kits short and needed to get them in. This, warts and all, approach meant that we attracted and retained people who thrived in that kind of chaos. They were there to stretch themselves and show tenacity, more than because they'd been furloughed and just needed a job. These are the kinds of personalities that a rapidly scaling business needs. They push the boundaries, they push themselves, and they make things happen with scarce resources and a fairly vague job description to follow. They see what needs to be done and get on with it. Not waiting for instruction or permission. They just run with it.

YDFM was brilliant at including us in pre-planning and keeping us informed about what was going on in the business.

They had to be circumspect about some things as NDAs would have to be signed before working on some big Hollywood, Netflix or Amazon project, so we wouldn't always get in-depth info, but we would get a heads up to prepare for a flurry of recruiting activity. The founders were also really open about any frustrations and worries. This is refreshing and can be rare when people often want to project that everything is wonderful and going swimmingly to external parties. In that way, they took me into their confidence and bared all (metaphorically speaking, of course!). This enabled me to work with the cold, hard facts and get the people that the business really needed because nothing was hidden from me at any time.

That's the power of embedding versus partnering. It's not about semantics. It's about results. From zero to 30 million turnover in 21 months is a fabulous result. We placed over 200 people at that time. And we placed the right people, largely because YDFM enabled us to work our magic.

Structuring the Relationship That Actually Works

So you're convinced that embedding your recruiter is the way to go. Brilliant! But how do you actually make this work in practice without creating chaos or confusion?

The key is having a clear structure with well-defined boundaries, expectations, and processes that everyone understands and commits to. Here's how to create a framework that delivers results:

Define Access and Involvement

Start by being crystal clear about how your recruiter will integrate with your team. Will they have access to your internal systems? Which meetings should they attend? Who will be their primary point of contact for day-to-day questions? The most successful embedded relationships I've seen include:

A regular presence in your workspace. Whether that's physical or virtual. Even if it's just one day a week in your office or a standing video call, this consistent face time is invaluable.

Direct access to hiring managers. And not just HR or a single gatekeeper. Your recruiter needs to build relationships with the people who will actually work with new hires.

Inclusion in strategic discussions. Particularly those related to growth plans, department restructures or new product or service launches. These conversations provide crucial context for future hiring needs. In my experience, our biggest client successes have occurred when I have been treated like one of the Senior Leadership Team. Privy to, and included in, board and strategic meetings and decision-making. This is possibly because I have absolutely no filter in calling out BS or bad ideas. This is why I'm not everyone's cup of tea to work with.

Establish Clear Communication Channels

Nothing kills recruitment momentum faster than communication breakdowns. Set up dedicated channels that ensure information flows quickly and clearly:

A shared project management tool. Whether it's Trello, Asana, or a purpose-built ATS, having a single source of truth for all recruitment activities eliminates confusion.

Regular 'finger on the pulse' meetings. Weekly at a minimum, during active hiring, with a structured agenda that covers progress updates, bottlenecks, and upcoming priorities.

Emergency protocols. Sometimes things go wrong, or unexpected opportunities arise. Define how urgent matters will be handled outside regular channels. We're dealing with people here, people!

Create Accountability Mechanisms

Accountability must run both ways for this relationship to succeed. This means:

Defined SLAs for both parties. Not just how quickly your recruiter should respond to you, but also how promptly you'll provide feedback on candidates or answer queries. And that your feedback has a certain level of detail. "They're a no" is not useful in refining selection.

Transparent metrics and reporting. Agree on what success looks like and how it will be measured upfront. Time-to-hire, quality-of-hire and candidate experience are good starting points.

Regular relationship reviews. Quarterly step-backs to assess what's working, what isn't and how the relationship can be optimised further.

One of my most successful client relationships involves a monthly "honest hour" where both sides can raise any frustrations or concerns without fear of damaging the relationship. This regular pressure release valve has prevented small issues from festering into relationship-ending problems.

Your Role in Making This Work (Yes, You Have One)

Here's an uncomfortable truth that most recruiters won't tell you: When recruitment goes wrong, it's often the client's fault. Or that's what many recruiters on LinkedIn would have you believe. And I've been one to say this in private, or at recruiter conferences where we all get to have a good old bitch and moan. The truth of the matter is, this is still the recruiter's fault. They've allowed it to happen. There have been many cases over the years where I haven't made all the expectations, responsibilities and boundaries absolutely clear. This is where it can fall down.

I can almost hear you spluttering into your coffee, but bear with me. The best recruiter in the world can't succeed if you're setting them up to fail. And many clients do exactly that, often without realising it. So, if you're going to work with somebody who is so eager to get your business and unwilling to assert their authority as the expert in this situation, then you need to take some responsibility for the results. You wouldn't take your car to a mechanic and then tell them how to fix it, would you? You also wouldn't refuse to let them examine it or run a diagnostic to gather all the relevant information before deciding on the best course of action.

If you want stellar results from your recruiter, you need to own your part of the process. Here's what that looks like:

Provide Genuine Access and Insight

Your recruiter can only represent what they truly understand. This means:

Sharing the unvarnished truth about your business. The good, the bad, and the occasionally ugly. If your tech stack is outdated or your office is in the middle of nowhere, hiding these facts only leads to disappointed new hires who quickly leave.

Making key people available for your recruiter to interview and understand. Your recruiter should know your team almost as well as you do. This also applies to hiring managers and senior leaders. Even the CEO. If everyone is too busy or too important to communicate with me and my team, then they may not be ready to hire well.

Offering context, not just requirements and explaining why a role exists, how it fits into the bigger picture, and what success looks like beyond a list of technical skills.

Commit to Responsive Feedback

Nothing kills a recruitment process faster than slow feedback. Top candidates are typically off the market within days, not weeks. This means:

Reviewing CVs within 24 hours. Your recruiter should make this process easier by pre-screening candidates and only sending those who are genuinely suitable.

Providing detailed feedback after interviews. Not just "not a fit" but specific reasons why, so your recruiter can refine their search.

Making decisions quickly. Having a streamlined internal approval process for making offers once you've found the right person.

I once worked with a client who took two weeks to decide on a candidate, only to discover they'd accepted another offer ten days earlier. That role remained unfilled for another three months, resulting in an estimated £40,000 in lost productivity for the business.

I've also had candidates reject an offer that took too long when they didn't have anything else on the table. The reason given? "I can't work in a place where the directors take that long to make a decision. Can you imagine how difficult it will be to get anything done when I need to move quickly, and a complex decision needs to be made?"

We've all heard the saying, "How you do anything is how you do everything", haven't we? Whether it's true or not, that's the perception.

Be Brutally Honest About Culture

Your company culture isn't what you put on your website or in your employee handbook. It's how things actually work on a day-to-day basis. Your recruiter needs to understand:

How decisions really get made in your organisation. Not the official process, but the actual one.

What behaviours get rewarded? Not what your values statement says, but what actually leads to promotion and recognition.

The unwritten rules that everyone knows but nobody talks about. Like whether 9 am really means 9 am, or if it's actually 9:30 am with a coffee in hand.

One client insisted they had a "flat structure with no hierarchy" until I pointed out that every decision seemed to require the founder's approval, and nobody would schedule meetings before 10 am because "that's when Sarah likes to start." The disconnect between their perceived culture and reality was causing significant retention issues.

If you recognise that there is a disconnect between your publicly communicated culture and actual culture, be honest about the work that you're going to do (or are doing) to make sure it aligns with reality. Culture change is an evolution that takes time. It can also cause ripples of frustration and sometimes ill will amongst existing teams. Any newcomer needs to know what they may be navigating.

The Transformative Power of Deep Understanding

When your recruiter truly understands your business, not just your immediate hiring needs but your vision, challenges, culture, and growth trajectory, they can deliver value that goes far beyond filling vacancies.

This deep understanding enables them to:

Spot potential issues before they become problems. Identifying that your engineering team is heavy on technical skills but light on leadership capabilities can potentially create issues as you scale.

Challenge your assumptions constructively. Perhaps that Head of Sales role you're desperate to fill could actually be better structured as two more focused positions.

Represent your employer brand authentically. Conveying not just what you do but why you do it, attracting candidates who connect with your mission.

Build talent pipelines ahead of need. Nurturing relationships with potential future hires even when you're not actively recruiting.

Why My Battle Scars Make Me Your Secret Weapon

There's a world of difference between recruiters who've only ever been recruiters and those who've sat where you're sitting now. As an entrepreneur who's built my own business, I understand the unique pressures you're facing in a way that most recruiters simply can't.

I know what it's like to:

Lie awake at 3 am, worrying about making payroll or whether that big client will renew.

Feel the crushing weight of responsibility for the livelihoods and futures of others.

Make difficult decisions with incomplete information because waiting for perfect clarity isn't an option.

Stretch every pound until the Queen (I know we've got the King now, but I just can't bring myself to accept his head on my money) is begging for mercy because cash flow is tight and every expense needs to justify itself.

Felt all the overwhelm, the crying at my desk, the imposter syndrome and crushing self-doubt. And then showing up as the happy, optimistic me for everyone else.

These experiences aren't theoretical for me. They live in reality. And they fundamentally change how I approach recruitment for my clients.

I understand that a bad hire isn't just an inconvenience; it can be a significant problem. It's a potentially existential threat to a growing business. I know that the opportunity cost of a lengthy recruitment process can be just as damaging as making the wrong hire. And I recognise that sometimes the perfect candidate on paper isn't the right person for your specific situation.

This perspective means I'm not just filling vacancies; I'm helping you build a team that can weather the storms of entrepreneurship alongside you. Because I've weathered those storms myself.

How My AuDHD Supercharges Your Recruitment

I spent most of my life not knowing why I saw patterns others missed, or why I could form such deep connections with clients and candidates when other recruiters struggled. Then came my diagnosis with AuDHD (Autism with ADHD), and suddenly, everything made sense.

What some might call neurodivergence, I call my secret weapon – and it's one that directly benefits you, my client. Whilst it can also be my kryptonite, it's always easier for me to show up in my full show pony regalia and smash the brief for someone else than it is for me. Sound familiar?

My autism gives me:

- Pattern recognition abilities that help me spot connections between seemingly unrelated skills or experiences in candidates' backgrounds.
- Hyperfocus on the details of your requirements, ensuring nothing gets missed or misinterpreted.
- A natural tendency toward systems thinking that helps me understand how each role fits into your broader organisational structure.

Meanwhile, my ADHD brings:

- Creative problem-solving when traditional recruitment approaches aren't yielding results.
- Genuine enthusiasm and passion that candidates can feel when I talk about your business.
- The ability to build rapid rapport with diverse personalities, which helps me connect with candidates who might be a perfect fit for your culture.

Together, these traits mean I don't just understand your business intellectually; I feel it. I become emotionally invested in your success in a way that neurotypical recruiters might find difficult to match.

When you share your vision with me, I don't just hear the words; I see the picture. I see the future you're describing in vivid detail. When you explain a challenge, I don't just acknowledge it; I feel the urgency and importance as if it were my own problem to solve.

This isn't about being "better" than other recruiters; it's about being different in ways that create unique value for entrepreneurs and growing businesses. It's about treating your business as if it were my own because, in many ways, that's exactly how I experience it.

You only have to see how involved I get in a film, TV series or book to understand that I immerse myself at a visceral level. My great-nephews and great-nieces can often be heard saying, "It's CGI!" as I'm breaking my heart over the *Planet of the Apes*. If I get this invested in a movie, imagine how invested I am in your business that affects real lives!

From Transaction to Transformation

Most recruitment relationships remain stubbornly transactional. A necessary evil rather than a strategic advantage. But it doesn't have to be this way.

When you embed the right recruiter into your team, structure the relationship thoughtfully, own your responsibilities in the process, and find someone who genuinely understands and cares about your business, recruitment transforms from a painful cost centre into a powerful driver of growth.

The right people brought into your business at the right time and for the right reasons can be the difference between stagnation and scale, between burnout and breakthrough, between a good business and a great one.

So stop treating recruitment as something you do occasionally when you're desperate. Start seeing it as a continuous, strategic function that deserves as much care and attention as your product development, marketing or financial planning.

Your business – and your sanity – will thank you for it.

Chapter 7
How to Make Your Recruiter Redundant

There comes a point in every growing business's journey when your relationship with your external recruiter needs to evolve. Perhaps you've reached that sweet spot where your team is humming along nicely, and you're not constantly scrambling to fill new positions. Or maybe you've grown so substantially that the mathematics of recruitment has shifted, and bringing the function in-house makes more financial sense. Either way, it's a milestone worth celebrating! If you're reading this chapter, you've likely navigated the treacherous waters of early-stage hiring and built a team that's helping your business thrive. The constant churn of recruitment has slowed, and you're thinking about what comes next.

Making your external recruiter "redundant" doesn't necessarily mean cutting ties completely. Rather, it's about transitioning to a new phase of your relationship, one that might involve less frequent engagement or a completely different approach to talent acquisition.

On more than one occasion, I've worked with businesses that reach a certain point in team growth when they feel they have sufficient internal resources to handle recruitment themselves. This often coincides with someone looking at the recruitment bill, because it can be really hefty at the beginning. Make sure you're a smart cookie who looks at value rather than cost. Spending between half a million and three-quarters of a million on agency fees sounds like an enormous amount in isolation. But if you were told you could grow turnover to £30 million for that, plus your wage costs, you probably wouldn't bat an eyelid.

It is, however, a spend that is probably unsustainable as growth is rarely linear and will undoubtedly plateau at some stage. The most successful businesses phase into the next era rather than deciding to handle all recruitment themselves immediately. I've seen so many times when internal people are handed the mantle of responsibility and are ill-equipped to do a good job, let alone the damage that is done by them taking the eye off the ball in their usual role. Even when dedicated internal recruiters are appointed, some rush to demonstrate how much they can save the business and commence campaigns and searches before they have the right process, technologies and pipelines in place. Reluctant to be seen to lean on their recruiters, they ignore or discard the talent pools and intel that have been created and nurtured during the initial scaling phase.

This can cost a business dear. When you embed your recruiter, make sure that your regular review and forecasting meetings include succession planning and what will trigger phasing out their daily involvement. Unless, of course, you decide to retain an external resource, rather than bring everything in-house. In this chapter, we'll explore how to recognise when you've reached this inflexion point, what your options are and how to make the transition as smooth as possible for everyone involved. Because let's be honest, your recruiter has been instrumental in getting you to this point, and maintaining that relationship (even in a different form) might still be valuable for your future growth.

Signs It's Time to Rethink Your Recruitment Approach

Before making any decisions about your recruitment strategy, it's important to recognise the signs that you've reached a turning point. Here are some indicators that it might be time to reconsider your current approach:

Your hiring volume has significantly decreased. If you've gone from making multiple hires every month to perhaps one or two per quarter, the economics of your recruitment strategy may need reassessment.

Your team has stabilised. You've filled all the critical positions on your organisational chart, and turnover has decreased to manageable levels.

You're spending a small fortune on recruitment fees. When you tally up what you've paid to external recruiters over the past year, the number makes your eyes water – and makes you wonder if there's a more cost-effective approach.

Your HR team has grown and developed. You now have internal HR professionals who understand your business and could potentially take on some recruitment responsibilities.

Your business has reached a certain scale. Research suggests that businesses with more than 50 – 100 employees often reach a tipping point where in-house recruitment becomes more economically viable.

You need more control over your employer brand. As your business matures, how you present yourself to potential candidates becomes increasingly important, and you want more direct control over this messaging.

If several of these signs resonate with you, it's likely time to consider your options for the next phase of your talent acquisition strategy.

Your Options: Finding the Right Model for Your Business

When it comes to evolving your recruitment approach, there's no one-size-fits-all solution. The right model depends on your business size, hiring needs, budget and growth projections. There will be many moving parts and factors to take into account. These will include things like what your future growth, hiring numbers and requirements are going to look like. And, while this may feel like you need a crystal ball at times, you can give yourself a bit of help by having a strategy in place, like I keep on banging on about. Your current resource and in-house expertise will play their part, as will budgetary constraints and appetite for creating another support function internally. Some business owners will decide to continue outsourcing certain tasks so that their team can focus on their main business-critical purposes and objectives. Or they simply value external input, not clouded by internal drivers (or politics), when it comes to important decisions like who joins the team.

Let's explore the main options:

Option 1: HR Team with Occasional Recruiter Support

This hybrid model works well for businesses that have stabilised their growth and make only occasional hires. Here's what it looks like:

Your internal HR team handles: job descriptions, internal job postings, employee referrals, initial candidate screening, interview coordination and onboarding.

External recruiters are engaged for: hard-to-fill positions, executive searches or when you need to hire multiple positions simultaneously.

This approach works particularly well when your hiring needs are sporadic or seasonal; you have a competent HR team that can handle basic recruitment functions; and you still occasionally need specialised recruitment expertise for certain roles. The main advantage here is flexibility, as you're not committed to the fixed costs of a dedicated recruitment function, but you still have access to professional recruitment support when needed.

Option 2: Dedicated In-House Recruiter

As your business grows, there comes a point where having a dedicated in-house recruiter becomes financially sensible. This typically happens when you're consistently making 15+ hires per year; you're spending more than the equivalent of one recruiter's annual salary on agency fees; and you want to develop a more sophisticated approach to talent acquisition.

An in-house recruiter brings several advantages:

Deep understanding of your culture. They live and breathe your company values every day, making them better equipped to identify candidates who will thrive in your environment.

Cost efficiency for frequent hiring. Once established, the fixed costs of an in-house recruiter are often lower than ongoing agency fees, especially if you're making multiple hires throughout the year.

Improved candidate experience. Direct communication between candidates and your company (rather than through an agency) often creates a more seamless and authentic experience.

Greater control over the recruitment process. You can develop standardised processes that align perfectly with your business needs and values.

The main challenge with this option is that a single in-house recruiter has limited bandwidth. If your hiring needs suddenly spike, you may still need external support. If they wane, you have a permanent salary on your headcount budget.

Option 3: Full Talent Acquisition Team

For larger businesses or those experiencing rapid growth, a full talent acquisition team might be the most effective solution. This typically includes a Talent Acquisition Manager or Director who oversees the strategy, multiple recruiters who specialise in different departments or types of roles, sourcers who focus specifically on finding passive candidates, and recruitment coordinators who handle the administrative aspects of the process. This model is generally appropriate when your company has 200+ employees, you're making

30+ hires annually, you want to develop sophisticated talent pipelines and employer branding, and you need specialised recruitment expertise across multiple departments.

The advantages of a full talent acquisition team include:

Strategic approach to talent. Rather than just filling vacancies, a talent acquisition team can develop long-term strategies to build talent pipelines and enhance its employer brand.

Scalability. With multiple team members, you can handle hiring surges without being overwhelmed or needing to engage external agencies.

Reduced hiring costs. While the upfront investment is significant, the per-hire cost typically decreases substantially compared to agency fees.

Future leadership pipeline. A talent acquisition team can focus not just on immediate needs but on building relationships with potential future leaders for your organisation.

The main drawback is the significant fixed cost, which may not be justifiable unless your hiring volume is consistently high.

Option 4: Me and My Team! (Or Somebody Else Who Does This Well)

The fourth option I offer to clients is embedding one of my teams as a full talent acquisition team within the client on a retained basis for six or twelve months initially, with the option to roll over the contract for as long as needed. This is similar to how we worked with YDFM, except for the billing mechanism.

My Six-Step Approach To Making The Transition

Once you've decided on the right model for your business, transitioning from your current approach requires careful planning. Here's how to make the shift as smooth as possible:

Step 1: Analyse Your Current Recruitment Metrics

Before making any changes, gather data on your current recruitment activities:

How many hires do you typically make per year?

What are you spending on recruitment fees?

Which roles are easiest/hardest to fill?

What's your average time-to-hire?

What's your quality-of-hire like?

This data will help you make an informed decision and establish benchmarks to measure the success of your new approach.

Step 2: Build a Business Case

If you're planning to bring recruitment in-house, you'll likely need to justify the investment to other stakeholders. Your business case should include:

- Current annual spend on recruitment agencies
- Projected costs of your proposed model (salaries, benefits, recruitment tools, etc.)
- Expected ROI and timeline
- Non-financial benefits (improved candidate experience, better cultural fit, etc.)
- Risks and mitigation strategies

Be realistic in your projections. The transition period may initially increase costs before you see savings.

Step 3: Have an Honest Conversation with Your Current Recruiter

If you've been working with an external recruiter who's helped you build your team, they deserve transparency about your plans. Schedule a conversation to discuss your changing needs and why you're considering a different approach. Discuss with them how you envision working together in the future (if applicable) and agree on a timeline for your transition. Make sure they are aware of any ongoing searches they should complete. Better still, get them to help recruit the incoming talent acquisition team for you. They are in a great place to share intel on what challenges and opportunities they've had in finding the right people for your business so far. A good recruiter will understand that business needs evolve and may even offer advice on your transition. Remember, maintaining this relationship could be valuable for future specialised hiring needs.

Step 4: Develop Your Internal Capabilities

Whether you're shifting responsibility to your HR team or building a dedicated talent acquisition function, you'll need to develop internal capabilities. If you're expanding the responsibilities of your HR team, you will need to provide training on recruitment best practices and have them develop standardised recruitment processes and templates. Investing in appropriate recruitment tools (ATS, job boards, etc.) and guidance on copywriting for job advertisements would also be beneficial. That is, unless you're going to get your marketing team involved in that, which isn't a bad idea. HR tends to cut and paste a job description into an advert, and it reads like the Shipping Forecast. Boring as fuck!

Many HR professionals also loathe doing recruitment. If you're hiring dedicated recruiters and creating a talent acquisition team, you need to define clear roles and responsibilities. Looking for recruiters with experience in your industry can be useful, as the good ones will have a great network of talent to tap into. You may consider whether agency recruiters might be good candidates. They won't come cheap, though, because the best will command excellent commission structures as well as a decent basic salary. Most importantly, you need to develop a comprehensive onboarding plan to get them up to speed quickly. If you've embedded your agency recruiter into your business, they can handle all of this for you.

Step 5: Implement Gradually

Rather than making a sudden switch, consider a phased approach. This means you start by bringing certain types of roles in-house while continuing to use agencies for others. You gradually reduce your reliance on external recruiters as your internal capabilities develop. You should always use metrics to track the effectiveness of your new approach and make adjustments as needed. It's really easy to think something is working well (or not so well) only to find that the data tells a very different story. Know how you will measure success. A good question to ask is, "How will we know this is working for us?" This gradual transition reduces risk and allows you to build confidence in your new model before making a full commitment.

Step 6: Maintain Relationships with External Recruiters

Even with an in-house function, maintaining relationships with trusted external recruiters is wise because they can provide support during hiring surges. They often have specialised networks for hard-to-fill roles, and they can offer market insights and salary benchmarking. They provide a backup option if an internal recruiter leaves.

Common Pitfalls and How to Avoid Them

As with any significant change, there are potential pitfalls in transitioning your recruitment approach. Here are some common challenges and how to address them:

Underestimating the complexity of recruitment. Many businesses assume that recruitment is simpler than it actually is. Avoid this by investing in proper training and tools for those who take on recruitment responsibilities. This is easily done because the process from the client side often looks like this: The client gives the recruiter the brief, and the recruiter presents some brilliant candidates within weeks or days. The client doesn't see the flurry of activity and outreach that happens. They don't see the hundreds of CVs that are sifted and the 10-hour days of back-to-back interviewing. They don't appreciate that the networks we can tap into have been developed and nurtured over the course of decades. It may not be rocket science, but we really do make it look too easy.

Losing access to specialist networks. In-house recruiters may not have the same depth of specialist networks as agency recruiters who focus on specific niches. Mitigate this by maintaining relationships with specialist agencies for hard-to-fill roles.

Creating a recruitment silo. In-house recruitment can sometimes become disconnected from broader business strategy. Prevent this by ensuring your recruitment function has visibility of and input into strategic business planning.

Inadequate technology. Many businesses try to save money by skimping on recruitment technology. Invest in a good Applicant Tracking System (ATS) and other tools that will make your in-house team more efficient.

Failing to measure success. Without clear metrics, it's hard to know if your new approach is working. Establish KPIs from the outset and regularly review performance against them.

When to Stick with External Recruiters or Your Embedded Talent Team

While this chapter focuses on transitioning away from heavy reliance on external recruiters, there are circumstances where continuing to use them makes perfect sense:

- For highly specialised roles where specific industry knowledge and networks are crucial
- During periods of unexpected growth when your internal team is at capacity
- For executive and leadership positions where discretion, extensive networks, and specialised assessment skills are valuable

- When expanding into new geographic markets where you lack local knowledge and connections
- For project-based or temporary recruitment needs that don't justify permanent headcount

The key is to be strategic about when and how you use external recruiters, rather than defaulting to them for every hiring need.

The Future of Your Recruitment Strategy

Your recruitment strategy should never be static. It needs to evolve as your business grows and changes. Even after transitioning to a new model, regularly reassess whether it's still serving your needs:

- Review your recruitment metrics quarterly.
- Solicit feedback from hiring managers and new hires.
- Stay informed about new recruitment technologies and approaches.
- Benchmark your practices against industry standards.
- Be prepared to adjust your model as your business continues to evolve.

Remember, the goal isn't to make your recruiter permanently redundant. It's to ensure you have the most effective, efficient approach to finding and securing the talent your business needs at each stage of its development.

Final Thoughts

Making your external recruiter "redundant", or more accurately, evolving your relationship with them, is a sign of success. It means you've reached a new stage in your business journey where your recruitment needs have changed. Whether you choose to bring recruitment fully in-house, develop a hybrid model, or simply change how you engage with external recruiters, the key is to make a conscious, data-driven decision that aligns with your business strategy and culture.

The recruitment landscape is constantly changing. The approach that works for you today may need to evolve again as your business continues to grow and transform. Stay flexible, keep measuring what matters and don't be afraid to adjust your strategy as needed. After all, building a remarkable business isn't about finding one perfect approach. It's about continuously adapting and evolving as you grow. Just like there's no such thing as a unicorn candidate, there's no perfect recruitment model that works for every business at every stage. The magic happens when you find the right approach for your business's current stage and remain open to adapting it as your needs evolve.

Here's to your success and to finding the recruitment approach that will take your business to the next level of growth!

Chapter 8
Common Pitfalls and Problems in Start-up Recruiting

Let's be brutally honest, recruitment is a minefield, and start-ups seem particularly adept at stepping on every explosive along the way. Perhaps it's the frenetic pace, the bootstrapped budgets or simply the fact that most founders are brilliant at their core business but have never had to build a team from scratch before.

Whatever the reason, I've spent nearly three decades watching start-ups make the same recruitment mistakes over and over again. These aren't just minor hiccups. They're business-threatening blunders that can derail your growth, drain your resources and in the worst cases, sink your company entirely.

The statistics are sobering: 90% of start-ups fail over the long term, with only about 10% achieving success. While there are many factors at play, poor hiring decisions rank among the most devastating. In fact, hiring mistakes account for 14%

of start-up failures. That's not a typo! One in seven start-up deaths can be traced back to building the wrong team.

But here's the good news. These pitfalls are entirely avoidable if you know what to look for. In this chapter, I'll walk you through the most common recruitment mistakes that start-ups make, show you the real-world impact of these errors and arm you with practical strategies to sidestep these traps altogether. Consider this your recruitment survival guide. In the start-up world, the team you build isn't just nice to have; it's the difference between becoming the next success story or becoming another statistic.

The Magnificent Seven: Start-Up Recruitment Mistakes That Will Haunt You

When it comes to recruitment blunders, start-ups display remarkable creativity. However, after years of observing these patterns repeat, I've identified seven deadly sins that seem particularly prevalent in the startup ecosystem. Let's dissect them one by one:

1. The Desperate Dash: Hiring Too Quickly

There's a particular brand of panic that sets in when start-ups begin to grow. Suddenly, there's too much work, too few hands, and everyone's drowning in tasks. The natural response? Hire someone. Anyone! And as quickly as humanly possible.

This desperation leads to rushed processes, skipped reference checks and gut-feel decisions that often end in tears. According to a study by Leadership IQ, 46% of new hires fail within the first 18 months, often due to rushed hiring processes. That's nearly half of all hires crashing and burning before they've even properly settled in.

2. The Culture Blindspot: Ignoring Fit for Skills

In the race to secure technical talent, many start-ups focus exclusively on skills and experience while completely overlooking cultural fit. This is a catastrophic error. A 2018 study found that 32% of new hires who quit within the first 90 days do so because of a lack of cultural fit.

Think about that for a moment. Nearly a third of early departures have nothing to do with ability and everything to do with alignment. In fact, 89% of hiring failures in the first 18 months are due to poor cultural fit, not a lack of skills.

Cultural misalignment doesn't just lead to turnover; it creates friction, reduces productivity and can poison your carefully cultivated company culture. I always tell my clients to recruit based on aptitude and attitude. If they have the aptitude to learn and the attitude to do so (and the sort of attitude that aligns with your culture), then you're more than halfway to success. Most things can be taught. Except for attitude.

3. The Unicorn Hunt: Unrealistic Expectations

Many start-ups draft job descriptions that would make even Spock raise an eyebrow. They want a technical genius who's also a brilliant communicator, an innovative thinker who rigidly follows processes, and someone willing to work for peanuts while delivering caviar results. This unicorn hunting leads to perpetually unfilled positions, or worse, hiring people who claim to be unicorns but turn out to be donkeys with an ice cream cone strapped to their heads.

As I mentioned in the introduction to this book, unicorns don't exist, at least not in the talent market. What you need instead is a team of brilliant misfits whose complementary strengths and weaknesses create a powerful whole.

4. The False Economy: Underinvesting in Talent

Start-ups are often obsessively frugal. Cash is the oxygen that keeps the business alive. But this frugality becomes counterproductive when it extends to underinvesting in talent.

Offering below-market salaries, skimping on benefits or trying to hire senior talent at junior rates is a false economy. A 2020 Glassdoor survey found that 45% of employees cited salary as a primary reason for leaving a job. High turnover is exponentially more expensive than competitive compensation.

Consider this sobering calculation: Hiring the wrong person can cost your company at least 30% of that person's first-year salary. For a £50,000 role, that's £15,000 down the drain. That doesn't count the opportunity cost, the impact on team morale, or the disruption to your business. This mindset can extend to handling (badly) your own recruitment to avoid placement fees.

If you've accessed funding, allocate a portion of it specifically for the recruitment and onboarding of the best talent you can find. If you're bootstrapping, make sure to prioritise hiring someone who can bring in business or someone who can take a lot off your plate, if you're the person best placed to generate new sales and customers. Invest in doing it right, rather than doing it cheaply.

5. The Recruitment Chaos: No Structured Process

Many start-ups approach recruitment with all the organisation of a nursery school fire drill. There's no clear process, no consistent interview questions, no defined evaluation criteria, and no ownership of the hiring decision.

This chaos leads to poor candidate experiences, inconsistent assessments and ultimately, bad hiring decisions. Without structure, you're essentially rolling the dice on every hire.

A chaotic hiring process doesn't just impact who you hire; it damages your employer brand. In today's connected world, candidates share their experiences widely. A disorganised or negative recruitment experience can leave candidates with a bad impression of your company, and word spreads quickly in the digital age.

While this was certainly the case in the very early days of hiring for YDFM, the fallout was somewhat mitigated by ensuring that all our candidates possessed the right character and resilience. We had one or two people who couldn't cope with all the changes. And where they really got it right was by working with the talented Vanessa Di Cuffa, who developed a strategic plan and mapped out what would likely be needed for the business to succeed. She wasn't just engaged because the founder, Dr. Riccardo Di Cuffa, is her brother!

6. The Mirror Effect: Hiring in Your Own Image

Founders often unconsciously hire people who remind them of themselves. Similar backgrounds, similar thinking styles, similar personalities. While comfortable, this approach creates dangerous blind spots and limits diversity of thought.

The mirror effect leads to homogeneous teams that may get along swimmingly but lack the cognitive diversity needed to solve complex problems and innovate effectively. It also frequently results in teams that don't represent your customer base, limiting your ability to understand and serve your market.

One of the most common examples I see of this is when a solo entrepreneur takes on their first hire. They want to spread the workload and work with somebody easy to work with and communicate with. Somebody who thinks along the same lines, and they can trust to take on many of the tasks. There are so many problems with this.

Many years ago, I worked with a woman who had a social media business that was starting to get really busy, and she was run ragged. She finally decided to bite the bullet and take on an employee. I advised her to look for someone who would be responsible for bringing in new clients and managing accounts, while she continued to excel in the areas she was already strong in. She was adamant that she wanted an all-rounder who she could train to also create social media posts and campaigns, because she sometimes had too much on her plate.

Things worked well for about six months as they were busy and both were focusing on existing clients, and it took pressure off the business owner. They were so busy that neither of them had time to do any business development, sales or find new clients. Then they lost one big contract because the client decided to bring digital marketing in-house and there wasn't enough work for both of them. Because neither of them was particularly proficient in sales, and there is a pipeline and time delay when you're starting from scratch, the new hire had to be made redundant. The business owner was devastated. They'd become friends, and she felt guilty like she'd let her down.

7. The Role Roulette: Poorly Defined Positions

"We need someone to help with marketing... and maybe some sales... oh, and they should be able to handle customer support too." Sound familiar? Start-ups often create vague, catch-all roles that set new hires up for failure from day one.

Without clear job descriptions, candidates can't accurately assess whether they're qualified for the role or if it aligns with their career goals. This leads to mismatched expectations and early departures. Not having a clear job description can be one of the biggest mistakes start-ups make when hiring. Even worse, poorly defined roles create confusion about responsibilities, leading to important tasks falling through the cracks or duplicate efforts wasting precious resources.

The Ripple Effect: How Poor Hiring Decisions Poison Your Business

Bad hires aren't just inconvenient. They're toxic to your business in ways that extend far beyond the immediate impact. And because the mistakes aren't always immediately obvious, they become costly to correct in terms of mental energy as well as money. The problems created can also be insidious and far-reaching; we often only discover the true extent of the problem much later. I'm sure we've all heard of at least one instance of when somebody has been on holiday or sick leave, and somebody else has found a whole pile of fuck-ups hidden in a drawer! Let's explore the true cost of poor recruitment decisions:

Financial Haemorrhage

The direct costs of a bad hire are staggering. Beyond the 30% of salary rule of thumb mentioned earlier, consider all the resources wasted:

- Recruitment costs (advertising, agency fees, time spent interviewing)

- Onboarding and training expenses
- Salary, benefits and equipment during their tenure
- Potential severance or legal costs upon departure
- Recruitment costs to replace them

For cash-strapped start-ups, this financial drain can be existential. Tony Hsieh, the famous CEO of Zappos, once estimated that bad hires cost his company over $100 million. For start-ups operating on tight budgets, even a fraction of such losses could be devastating.

Productivity Paralysis

A single poor hiring decision can lead to a 36% drop in productivity. This productivity drain doesn't just affect the underperforming employee; it ripples through the entire team.

Other team members must pick up the slack, diverting their attention from their own responsibilities. Managers spend disproportionate time coaching and correcting employees who are struggling. Projects get delayed, deadlines are missed, and momentum stalls.

In the worst cases, the entire company can become fixated on managing the problems created by a bad hire rather than driving the business forward.

Cultural Contamination

Company culture isn't just about ping pong tables and free snacks. It's the invisible operating system that guides how work gets done. One toxic hire can corrupt this culture with remarkable speed.

Negative attitudes spread like viruses. Poor work ethic becomes normalised. Trust erodes. The collaborative spirit that drives innovation gives way to politics and self-preservation.

Once cultural contamination sets in, it's extraordinarily difficult to eradicate. As the saying goes, "Culture eats strategy for breakfast," and a bad hire with a side of toxicity can devour your carefully cultivated culture in a single sitting.

Reputation Damage

In today's connected world, your reputation as an employer is more visible than ever. Disgruntled employees don't suffer in silence. They leave scathing reviews on Glassdoor, vent on social media and warn their networks away from your company.

This reputational damage makes it harder to attract quality candidates in the future, creating a downward spiral where each subsequent hire is drawn from an increasingly limited talent pool.

Leadership Distraction

Perhaps the most insidious impact of poor hiring decisions is the distraction they create for leadership. Start-up founders and executives should focus on vision, strategy, and growth, rather than constantly putting out fires caused by poor hiring decisions.

Every hour spent managing performance issues, mediating conflicts or recruiting replacements is an hour not spent on activities that drive the business forward. This opportunity cost is impossible to calculate but potentially limitless in its impact.

Bullet-proofing Your Recruitment

Now that we've thoroughly warned you about the consequences of poor hiring decisions, let's discuss solutions. Here are practical strategies to avoid the common pitfalls and build a team that propels your start-up forward.

Slow Down to Speed Up

Yes, you're in a hurry. Yes, that position needed to be filled yesterday. But rushing the hiring process is a false economy that will cost you dearly in the long run.

Implement a structured hiring process with well-defined job descriptions, thorough interviews and reference checks. This will help ensure that you find candidates who are not only skilled but also a good cultural fit for your start-up.

Create a hiring plan that includes timelines, roles, and responsibilities. Use a structured interview process with the same questions at each stage to ensure consistent answers. Conduct reference checks and get feedback from previous employers. Conduct thorough background checks to identify any potential red flags.

Remember, it's better to have a position vacant for a few extra weeks than to fill it with the wrong person who will set you back months.

Shameless plug: An experienced recruiter like me and my team can do all of this a lot more quickly and effectively than most of you can. We already have the systems, processes, networks, people, and know-how in place. You'd go straight to a mechanic if your car broke down, wouldn't you? You wouldn't even entertain learning how to fix it, buying all the tools and diagnostics, and then doing it yourself.*

*I actually did exactly this when I bought a 1972 Series 3 Land Rover off eBay and found out what a money-pit they can be. I went to night classes at Dudley College to do a light vehicle maintenance and repair course and even got a VRQ Level 1 qualification. I had lots of fun fixing it. Then it was stolen from my drive a few months after I'd got it through its latest MOT. So, while it was fun and I learned new skills, I wouldn't recommend taking a year to become proficient in recruiting the right team, as you'll likely hinder (or even hijack) your growth. Especially if, after all that effort, some bastard comes along and steals them off you.

Define Your Culture Before You Hire For It

You can't hire for cultural fit if you haven't defined what your culture is. Take the time to articulate your company's values, mission and working style before you start recruiting.

During the interview process, assess candidates for cultural fit by asking questions that explore their values, work style and preferences. This will help you identify individuals more likely to thrive in your start-up's unique environment.

Define your company culture by clearly outlining your mission, values and work style so you know what kind of team members will thrive. Include culture-based interview questions about candidates' preferred work environment, collaboration style and problem-solving approach. Get team input by involving key employees in the hiring process to assess cultural fit from multiple perspectives.

Most people aren't actually very good at interviewing, no matter what they think. There is both an art and a science to getting to the nub of a person and their motivations and values. I could write a whole book on just this. I've also created a course for those who want to improve their skills. You can find it at www.recruitrecruit.co.uk in the resources section.

People tend to spend the majority of the interview assessing skills and experience with a cursory chat about the person. When they do turn the conversation to the individual as a person, they talk about hobbies and interests and rarely explore what really makes them tick and what their values and attitudes to certain things are. Another thing I've noticed is that people (even many recruiters) interview for the job specification. This creates a whole load of bias and only gets you a one-dimensional narrative based on the requirements of the job.

Prioritise the Right Roles at the Right Time

Not all positions are created equal, and hiring for the wrong roles at the wrong time is a common mistake for start-ups. Focus on roles that are critical for immediate business growth and consider outsourcing functions like HR, accounting, and IT support to reduce costs.

Use freelancers or contractors for short-term or specialised projects before committing to full-time hires. This approach provides flexibility as you determine exactly what you need in a permanent role.

As I've mentioned in previous chapters, consider whether an interim solution might be more appropriate than a permanent hire, especially for roles that are likely to evolve rapidly as your business grows.

Invest in Competitive Compensation

Yes, budget constraints are real, but so is the cost of turnover and bad hires. Research market rates for your hiring roles and offer competitive salaries and benefits. If cash is tight, get creative with your compensation package. Consider offering equity, flexible working arrangements, professional development opportunities or other non-monetary benefits that might appeal to your target candidates.

Remember, the goal isn't to be the highest-paying employer in your sector. It's to offer a fair package that attracts and retains the right talent for your business.

Create a Consistent, Structured Recruitment Process

Implement a structured interview process with a consistent framework for decision-making that applies to all candidates. This should include:

- Clear job descriptions that outline not just responsibilities and requirements, but also how the position contributes to your company's mission and growth

- A defined interview process with standard questions and evaluation criteria
- Multiple interviewers (who know what they're looking for and how to get the best out of an interviewee) to get diverse perspectives
- Practical assessments or work sample tests to evaluate skills in action
- Thorough reference checks, including both provided references and "backdoor" references through mutual connections

Sam Altman of OpenAI recommends having candidates "audition" by doing real work for 1 to 2 days. This approach provides a more accurate assessment of a candidate's skills and work style than traditional interviews alone, but it isn't always practical. And you must pay people for their time!

Prioritise Diversity of Thought

Actively work to build a team with diverse backgrounds, experiences and thinking styles. This diversity isn't just about ticking boxes; it's about creating a team that can approach problems from multiple angles and develop innovative solutions.

Be aware of your own biases in the hiring process. Consider implementing blind resume/CV reviews or structured interviews to minimise the impact of unconscious bias.

Remember, you're not building a team of clones; you're assembling a group of complementary individuals who can collectively achieve what none could accomplish alone.

Define Roles with Crystal Clarity

Develop detailed job descriptions that clearly outline the role, responsibilities, and expectations. Be specific about:

- Key responsibilities and tasks
- Required skills and experience
- Performance metrics and success criteria
- Reporting relationships and team interactions
- Growth and development opportunities

Clear role definitions help candidates self-select appropriately and set new hires up for success from day one. They also prevent the confusion and frustration that arise when expectations are misaligned.

The Founder's Mindset: Final Thoughts on Recruitment Success

As we conclude this exploration of start-up recruitment pitfalls, I would like to leave you with a perspective shift that may be the most valuable takeaway of all.

The most successful founders I've worked with don't see recruitment as a necessary evil or a distraction from their "real work." They view it as one of their most critical strategic functions and perhaps the most important lever they can pull to determine their company's success.

Sam Altman suggests founders should spend "between a third and a half of your time hiring" after achieving product-market fit. Up to half your time should be dedicated to finding and securing the right people for your team.

This might seem excessive, especially when you're juggling a thousand other priorities. But consider this: Every other aspect of your business – your product, marketing, operations, and culture – will be built and executed by the team you assemble. Get the team right and everything else becomes possible. Get it wrong and nothing else matters.

So approach recruitment not as a distraction but as your primary job. Be as strategic, thoughtful and rigorous about building your team as you are about building your product.

Invest the time and resources necessary to get it right, because the alternative – dealing with the fallout of poor hiring decisions – is infinitely more costly.

Remember, the best start-ups aren't built on brilliant ideas alone; they're built on brilliant teams that execute those ideas with passion, skill and alignment. Your recruitment strategy isn't just about filling seats; it's about creating the engine that will drive your business forward.

And if you're feeling overwhelmed by the complexity and importance of this task, take heart. The very fact that you're reading this book means you're already ahead of most founders. You're arming yourself with the knowledge and strategies needed to avoid the common pitfalls and build a team that can help you realise your vision.

The path to start-up success is rarely straight or smooth, but with the right team beside you, even the most challenging obstacles become surmountable. Choose wisely, hire deliberately, and watch your business transform as a result.

And, if you're concerned about doing it alone, let's have a conversation at www.recruitrecruit.co.uk about how I can help you with it.

Chapter 9
Building a High-Performance Team

Let's have a moment of radical honesty: Building a high-performance team in a start-up or scale-up is not for the faint-hearted. Forget the Instagrammable office plants and the beanbags. What actually matters is the people you bring in, how they work together and whether they're genuinely up for the wild ride that is start-up life. Spoiler: Not everyone is.

This chapter is your no-nonsense guide to assembling a team that doesn't just "get the job done" but propels your business to new heights. We'll delve into how to spot and win over top talent, why even the most impressive CVs can fail in a start-up, the make-or-break importance of cultural fit, and the practical tools for transforming a group of individuals into a high-performing, mission-driven team.

Identifying and Attracting Top Talent

First things first: Top talent is not just about technical brilliance or a string of fancy job titles. In the start-up world, you're looking for people who are adaptable, resilient and genuinely excited by ambiguity. You want the ones who see a blank canvas and reach for the paint, not the ones who ask where the instruction manual is.

So how do you attract these lunatics who thrive in the chaos and create structure and success?

Be clear on your passion and purpose. Somewhere out there are people who get as excited and revved up about the same things you do. If you can articulate what your purpose is all about, you will speak directly to these people.

Admittedly, the Your Doctor Film & Media gig got off to a start through necessity, catalysed by a global pandemic, rather than being a passion project. However, with everyone confined to isolation, people were consuming more TV and film content to alleviate boredom and loneliness. Tapping into this greater purpose made sure that the people on board felt like they were helping everyone in some way. That's one of the reasons why everybody continuously went above and beyond, working some insane hours and dealing with the demands of Hollywood and the UK filmmaking industry. Most importantly, in my opinion, is that they kept the national treasure, Dame Maggie Smith, safe while working on *Downton Abbey.*

Craft an irresistible employer brand. Your employer brand is your shop window. It's what tells candidates why they should pick you over a big-name corporation with a bigger pay cheque. Be loud and proud about your mission, your values, and what makes your culture unique. Use your website, social media and even your job ads to showcase what it's really like to work at your company. Most importantly, look at what you want to achieve.

Pay attention to the strength of your personal brand. If people get your vibe, catch your enthusiasm, and respect or admire what you are doing, they will buy into your journey, even if the product or service isn't something that would usually spark their interest. Don't hide behind your brand or have a faceless website that doesn't introduce you or your team. Most people want to get a feel for who they will be working for and with. Let's face it, if you got an interview at the one company in the world you would (figuratively) kill to work for and the hiring manager, CEO, or Founder you'd be working for was an utter dickhead (dickheads are gender neutral), you would probably decline any offer. Or accept, learn enough to make selling your soul worthwhile, and then leave at the earliest opportunity.

Leverage your network. Personal recommendations and employee referrals are gold dust. People who already believe in your mission are likely to know others who'll be a great fit too.

This is the part where I always include a warning about working with friends and family. This can often work really well, allowing you to tap into a resource of support, loyalty, and trust, as well as their commercial and operational expertise.

It can also turn into the stuff of nightmares.

From experience, people can get weird when money and success come into play. Learn from my experience, because I haven't always learned the first time and have had at least two separate occasions when working with so-called friends ended up costing me money, time, progress, and a lot of sleep.

If you're going to work with friends or family, make it absolutely explicit that this is a business relationship and is separate from your familial or friendship connection. Make sure that you have formal contracts and agreements in place, as you would with anybody else. Also, make sure that you put *everything* in writing when discussing anything. You'd be amazed at how many people have a different interpretation of the agreement when it comes to them getting more money out of you. I don't even think many of them do this knowingly. They're convinced that it is what was agreed and that *you* are now trying to cheat them. I lost out financially because I decided to just pay and keep the friendship. With my ex-business partner, I did that, and I lost the friendship, as well as three others that meant much more to me anyway. As they say, you learn who your true friends are when shit like this goes down. Especially the ones who call in to find out what the story is before taking someone else's version of events without any conversation with you.

Offer more than money. You might not be able to match an FTSE 100 salary, but you can offer equity, flexible working arrangements, real responsibility, and the opportunity to make a visible impact. Setting clear milestones in place for improved earning potential provides everyone with a goal to strive for.

Top talent wants to be part of something meaningful, not just another cog in a giant machine. You can attract top talent despite being a small organisation. I've seen many smaller businesses pass up the opportunity to hire a really experienced, senior-level person because of their fears. They're scared that the person will know more than they do and think they're stupid. They're scared they will take over and their baby won't belong to them anymore. They're scared that they will leave the minute a better-paying opportunity arises. If I hear "they're overqualified" one more time, I think I'll scream. It's short-sighted.

The most successful founders get people who are more experienced and knowledgeable in their posts as soon as possible. Hire people you can learn from rather than ones you need to teach.

Be transparent about the journey. Don't sugar-coat the challenges. The right people will be energised by the reality of start-up life, not put off by it. Talk about the challenges and doubts you've had, too. We all know that founding and running a business isn't all shiny success like we see on LinkedIn and social media all the time. It's also about self-doubt, sleepless nights worrying about how you're going to pay everyone and being eyeball-burningly knackered because you're working all the time, or thinking about the business when you're not in the business.

Why Not Everyone Thrives in a Start-Up (Even If They're Brilliant)

Here's a truth bomb: Some people are simply not cut out for start-up or rapid scale-up environments, regardless of how dazzling their skills or experience may be. And that's absolutely fine! The start-up world is a unique beast. It's fast-paced, often chaotic and requires everyone to wear several hats (sometimes all at once).

What Makes Start-Up Life So Different?

Ambiguity is the norm. There's rarely a clear process, and you'll often be building the plane as you're flying it. Weirdos like me love this shit. Most people do not.

Roles are fluid. One minute you're leading a strategy session; the next, you're fixing the printer or answering customer queries. On more than one occasion, I found Pete Watts, CEO of Your Doctor Film & Media, emptying the bins at the Windsor HQ because everyone else was busy, and even when they had a sizeable team.

Pace is relentless. Deadlines shift, priorities change, and yesterday's plan might be obsolete by lunchtime.

Failure is part of the process. You'll make mistakes. Lots of them. The key is learning fast and moving on.

Some people thrive in this environment. They love the adrenaline, the autonomy and the chance to shape something from scratch. Others find it stressful, disorienting or just plain exhausting. And that's OK! The trick is to figure out which camp your candidates fall into before you hire them.

How do you do that? Ask about their appetite for change and ambiguity. Get them to share examples of when they've had to adapt quickly or work without a roadmap.

When recruiting for Client Relationship Managers at Your Doctor Film & Media, I had two candidates who repeatedly asked for a job description to prepare for the interview. I explained that we didn't yet have a formal job description; if we did, it would probably look different within three days of starting, so the overview I'd already given them would have to suffice. When I got another email asking whether the job description had been confirmed yet, I withdrew them from the process. They wouldn't have lasted five minutes and would have been miserable and stressed every minute of the day. Their need for a clearly defined structure and detail demonstrated that they would not be well-suited to the start-up environment. They would also have been very likely to want to run everything by someone before doing anything to make sure they weren't doing anything wrong. We needed people who would just get on with something, confident in their own ability to work it out if something went wrong, because nobody had time to babysit new starters at this stage.

Give them a real-life challenge. See how they approach a messy, open-ended problem. If there is any hesitation or their response indicates that they need to get all the operational ducks in a row before tackling the actual challenge head-on, then this is a red flag. Ask how they will deal with things that go wrong. If they approach it by mitigating risk to make sure things don't go wrong in the first place, rather than a "this is how I'll put the fire out and this is how I clean up after the fire" approach, then this is also a red flag.

Be honest about what start-up life is really like. If they flinch, they're probably not the right fit. Don't dismiss these red flags just because you really like the person and they have some valuable skills to bring to the table. Be honest and say they could be a perfect fit for the business in 6 to 12 months' time, when you've got your shit together a bit more, and that structure will enable them to thrive with you rather than survive in it.

Your business will need individuals like these. Just not right now.

At best, these individuals persevere until the structure and processes are in place, but they are so stressed and tired from it all that they rarely perform at their best and often fade into background roles. They start to resent relative newcomers getting promotions and recognition, and do little more than what is required of them according to the job specification (that you now have in place). At worst, they leave and talk about their experiences. Rarely, if ever, do they say that they weren't cut out to work in a dynamic, ever-changing start-up environment. What they will say is the place was a disorganised sack of shit and the founder didn't know what they were doing from one minute to the next, "always changing their mind and the goalposts." If that's their perspective, my friend, then that will be their reality.

The Importance of Cultural Fit and Shared Vision

Skills get you in the door. Cultural fit and shared vision keep you in the building.

In a small, fast-paced team, every new hire has a significant impact. One person out of sync with your values or working style can throw the whole dynamic off. That's why cultural fit isn't just a "nice to have." It's mission-critical!

We often bandy about the terms "company culture" and "cultural fit," but what does it really mean, and how do we find out who will fit in or improve the mix? Here's an overview and a few pointers:

What Does Cultural Fit Really Mean?

Shared values and behaviours. It's about more than just getting along; it's about believing in the same things and approaching work in compatible ways.

Alignment with your mission. People who genuinely care about your vision will go the extra mile, especially when times get tough.

Communication style and work ethic. Do they prefer direct feedback? Are they comfortable with autonomy? Do they thrive on collaboration or need more structure?

Cultural fit isn't about hiring clones. In fact, diversity of background, perspective, and thought is crucial for innovation and resilience. But everyone needs to buy into the same core values and vision, or you'll spend more time firefighting than growing.

So, now we understand what it's all about. How, then, do you determine whether someone is a good cultural fit for you and your business? And, it's not about getting a load of cookie-cutter people in place. Diversity is good for businesses, and people can have very different behaviours in all sorts of ways, yet still fit with your culture because your values and vision align.

How Do You Assess Cultural Fit?

Define your culture clearly. Make sure everyone on your team can articulate your values, mission and what "great" looks like in your environment.

Incorporate culture into your hiring process. Ask values-based questions, run team-based interviews and let candidates spend time with their potential colleagues.

Use behavioural assessments. Tools and surveys can help you objectively measure alignment with your culture.

Involve the team. Peer interviews are a great way to test chemistry and get buy-in from existing team members.

You must make sure that everyone involved in the interview and selection process is aware of their responsibilities.

Interviews should be a mix of competency, behavioural styles, and understanding values and motivations. I could write a whole book on just this and have created an online course for those who want a comprehensive and cost-effective solution to equip themselves and their teams to prevent costly hiring mistakes. Check out the resources page at www.recruitrecruit.co.uk for this and other courses and resources you might find useful.

Techniques for Fostering a High-Performance Team Environment

So, you've attracted the right people and made sure they're a good fit. Now what? Building a high-performance team is an ongoing process, not a one-time event. This is one of the reasons why having a strategy in place is essential. If you're hiring reactively and in a silo, then you're hiring for a role, rather than for the business as a whole. Even when you have this right, you then need to create an environment in which everyone can bring their best, thrive, and shine, progress their purpose and passion, and build their vision. Here's how to keep your crew firing on all cylinders:

Create a Shared Sense of Purpose

High-performing teams are united by a clear, compelling vision. Make sure everyone knows not just what you're doing, but why you're doing it.

- Communicate the vision regularly. Use stories, team meetings, and even your office walls to keep the mission front and centre.
- Connect individual roles to the bigger picture. Help each person understand how their work contributes to moving the business forward.

Set Clear Goals and Expectations

Ambiguity is great for creativity, but it's a nightmare for productivity.

- Define roles and responsibilities. Make sure that everyone is aware of what's expected of them and each other.
- Set measurable targets. Use OKRs (Objectives & Key Results), KPIs (Key Performance Indicators), or whatever acronym floats your boat, but make sure progress is visible and celebrated.

Foster Open Communication and Feedback

High-performing teams talk. A lot. But more importantly, they listen.

- Establish regular check-ins. Weekly one-to-ones, team stand-ups and retrospectives keep everyone aligned and surface issues early.

- Encourage honest feedback. Create a culture where people feel safe to speak up, admit mistakes and challenge ideas without fear.

Empower and Trust Your Team

Micromanagement is the enemy of high performance.

- Give people autonomy. Let them own their projects and make decisions within their sphere.
- Recognise and reward initiative. Celebrate not just results, but the behaviours and risks that drive innovation.

Invest in Growth and Development

The best teams are always learning.

- Offer training and mentoring. Support both technical and soft skill development.
- Encourage knowledge sharing. Run internal workshops, cross-functional projects and "lunch and learn" to spread expertise.
- Create clear career paths. Show your team how they can grow with the business. This keeps ambition inside your company, not outside it.

Build Diversity and Inclusion Into Your DNA

Diversity isn't just a buzzword; it's a performance multiplier.

- Seek out different perspectives. Make diversity a priority in your hiring and team-building.
- Create an inclusive environment. Make sure that everyone's voice is heard and that their contributions are valued.

Celebrate Success (Big and Small)

Recognition fuels motivation.

- Acknowledge achievements. Whether it's a shout-out in a meeting, a team lunch or a simple thank you, make recognition a habit.
- Celebrate progress, not just perfection. High performance is about continuous improvement, not unattainable standards.

Final Thoughts: The Real Secret to High-Performance Teams

Here's the truth: There's no magic formula, no one-size-fits-all blueprint. High-performance teams are built on clarity, trust, shared purpose and a relentless commitment to learning and growing together. It's messy, it's hard work, and it's absolutely worth it.

Remember, your goal isn't to find a mythical "perfect" hire. It's to assemble a group of imperfect-but-brilliant humans who share your vision and are willing to build something extraordinary, together. Get the right people on the bus, create the right environment and watch as your start-up transforms from a scrappy idea into a high-performing powerhouse.

So, roll up your sleeves, get started, and build the team that will take your business to the next level. The journey won't be easy, but with the right crew, it'll be one hell of a ride.

And, if you're still not sure you have the time, skills, or inclination to do it yourself, give me a shout at www.recruitrecruit.co.uk.

Chapter 10
Sustaining Growth and Preparing for the Future

Congratulations! You've built something remarkable. A business that's growing fast, attracting top talent, and making waves in your industry. But here's the truth that most entrepreneurs don't want to hear: Growth isn't a finish line; it's a marathon. And like any marathon, it requires planning, resilience, and a clear strategy to maintain momentum without burning out or losing your way.

In this chapter, I'll share the essential strategies for sustaining rapid growth, planning for future recruitment needs and evolving your recruitment practices as your business scales. Because if you're serious about building something that lasts, you need to think beyond today's wins and prepare for the long haul.

Strategies for Sustaining Rapid Growth

First, let's discuss how to maintain momentum once the initial burst of growth has slowed from an adrenaline-fueled sprint to a steady pace. Sustaining growth isn't about pushing harder; it's about working smarter and building a foundation that can handle the inevitable bumps in the road.

Planning for Future Recruitment Needs

Growth isn't just about today's hires; it's about tomorrow's talent pipeline. The key is proactive planning. You should always anticipate your future needs before they become urgent, or have someone responsible for this. At this stage, you will probably need a Chief People Officer as well as a Senior HR Lead.

While both the Chief People Officer (CPO) and the HR Director sit at the top table of people management, the two roles are far from interchangeable. The CPO is the architect of the organisation's overall people strategy, a true C-suite executive who shapes and drives the culture, talent agenda, and long-term vision for how people power the business. This is a role rooted in strategy, not just operations. The CPO works shoulder-to-shoulder with the CEO and fellow executives, acting as a trusted advisor and ensuring that every people-related initiative is tightly aligned with business objectives. They're the ones championing leadership development, succession planning, and a people-first culture that supports both growth and resilience. Their remit is broad, stretching across the entire company, and their influence is felt in every corner of the business, from the boardroom to the break room.

In contrast, the HR Director is the operational powerhouse of the HR world. They're responsible for ensuring the day-to-day operations of HR run smoothly, including recruitment, training, compliance, employee relations, and the implementation of HR policies. Their focus is tactical and departmental, ensuring that the wheels don't come off the HR wagon and that the business remains compliant and efficient. While HR Directors may contribute to strategic discussions, their primary responsibility is to oversee the execution of HR strategies at the functional level, supporting department managers, and handling the practicalities of people management.

The difference in organisational impact is clear. The CPO has a company-wide, strategic influence, reporting directly to the CEO or even the board, and is involved in shaping the culture and direction of the business at the highest level. The HR Director, meanwhile, typically reports to the CPO or another senior executive, and their impact is felt most strongly within the HR department itself. They're the ones implementing the policies, managing the HR team, and ensuring that the people strategy devised at the top actually gets delivered on the ground.

When it comes to responsibilities, the CPO is focused on the big picture: developing and implementing strategies for engagement, culture, leadership, and change management. They're thinking about the future, including succession planning, organisational health, and how to stay ahead of the curve. The HR Director, on the other hand, is focused on the present: overseeing recruitment, ensuring compliance with employment law, managing the HR team, and addressing the day-to-day needs of the business.

Naturally, the skills and experience required reflect these different focuses. The CPO needs a blend of deep HR expertise, strategic vision, and the gravitas to influence at the board level. They're change agents, culture champions, and business partners all rolled into one. The HR Director, meanwhile, must be a master of HR operations, with a keen eye for compliance, process, and people management. They need to be strong leaders in their own right, but their influence is most keenly felt in the smooth and efficient operation of HR processes.

In essence, the Chief People Officer is the strategic driver of people and culture, shaping the business's future from the highest level. The HR Director is the operational expert, ensuring that the people strategy is implemented flawlessly on a day-to-day basis. Both are vital, but their impact, focus, and influence are worlds apart.

From a people and talent perspective, they (and you) will need to make sure that the following tasks are all handled effectively:

Conduct workforce planning. Regularly review your strategic goals and map out what roles and skills you'll need in the next 6, 12, and 24 months. For example, if you're expanding into new markets, you'll need regional managers, compliance experts, and support staff ready to go.

Create talent pipelines. Don't wait until a vacancy appears; nurture relationships with potential candidates through talent pools, alumni networks, and industry events. Continue engaging with passive candidates so you're not starting from scratch when the time comes to hire.

Develop succession plans. Identify high-potential internal talent and prepare them for leadership roles. This reduces the risk of disruption when key team members move on or are promoted.

Align recruitment with business milestones. Use your growth roadmap to schedule hiring campaigns around major launches, product releases, or market entries. This ensures you have the right people in place at the right time.

Leverage data and analytics. Use workforce analytics to identify patterns, such as high turnover in certain roles or departments, and address underlying issues before they escalate.

How to Evolve Recruitment Practices as You Scale

As your business grows, your recruitment process must evolve from a reactive to a strategic approach, from ad hoc to a structured one. Here's how to do it:

Standardise and Automate

Implement clear, repeatable hiring processes. Use ATS (applicant tracking systems), AI screening tools*, and online assessment platforms to handle routine tasks. This not only speeds up the hiring process but also enhances the candidate experience and reduces bias.

*This is a bit controversial and subject to much debate within the talent and recruitment sector. I believe that the value you can derive from AI screening tools is largely dependent on the volume and scale of your hiring projects, as well as how effectively you prompt and utilise the available AI tools. Part of me thinks that good recruitment is all about people, and the human touch throughout the process is essential. The other part knows all too well how impossible it can be to stay on top of all the applications (especially when people don't always read the job adverts properly and apply for anything, whether they're qualified or not).

Build a Talent Acquisition Team

At a certain point, relying solely on external recruiters or ad-hoc hiring won't cut it. Consider establishing an in-house Talent Acquisition team. These will be dedicated professionals who understand your culture, your needs, and your growth plans. They can develop employer branding, manage pipelines, and ensure consistency across all aspects of the organisation. If you only need these on a project basis and not a full-time, permanent basis, then you can outsource to someone like me and my team.

Develop a Candidate Experience Strategy

Your reputation as an employer is everything. Create a seamless, transparent, and engaging candidate journey. Communicate clearly, provide feedback, and keep candidates informed. A positive experience attracts top talent and turns applicants into brand ambassadors.

I can't tell you how many candidates I've had over the years who have turned down job offers based on the length of time it takes to get a decision, or the amount of time spent faffing about in the recruitment process. The old adage, "How you do anything is how you do everything," also applies to your recruitment process.

Invest in Employer Branding

As you scale, your employer brand becomes your most valuable asset. Showcase your culture, values, and success stories on social media, your website, and at industry events. The stronger your brand, the easier it is to attract high-calibre candidates. Remember that you must demonstrate all the things you extol in your daily operations. These things must run through the very fibre of the business.

Foster a Culture of Continuous Improvement

Regularly review your recruitment metrics. These include metrics such as time-to-hire, quality-of-hire, and candidate satisfaction. Then refine your approach. Stay ahead of industry trends and be willing to experiment with new sourcing channels, interview techniques, and onboarding methods.

Preparing for the Future: The Long Game

Growth is exciting, but it's also unpredictable. The companies that thrive are those that prepare for different scenarios, whether it's a sudden market downturn, a new competitor, or a technological breakthrough.

Take control with scenario planning. Map out best-case, worst-case, and most likely futures, and develop contingency plans. For example, if a key client drops off, do you have the talent and resources ready to pivot quickly?

Invest in leadership development. As your team expands, so does the need for strong leaders who can sustain your culture and drive innovation. Building a leadership pipeline ensures you won't be caught flat-footed when rapid growth demands new management.

Stay agile and adaptable. The business landscape is constantly shifting. Regularly revisit your growth strategy, recruitment plans, and operational processes. Flexibility is the secret weapon of resilient, scalable businesses.

Build a learning organisation. Encourage experimentation, feedback, and continuous improvement. The more your team learns, the better equipped you'll be to navigate future challenges.

I always advise my clients to hire based on aptitude to learn and attitude to learning. You can teach most people most things. You cannot teach or train an attitude. Well, you can, but it's painful! It takes a lot of time and energy, and it's easier all around if you get somebody with the right attitude in the first place. There is also the danger that somebody with the wrong attitude will piss off everybody else around them, and you end up with bigger problems.

Final Words: Growth Is a Journey, Not a Destination

Sustaining growth and preparing for the future isn't about quick fixes or magic bullets. It's about building a resilient, adaptable organisation that can ride the waves of change without capsizing.

Start by laying a solid foundation: Clarify your vision, invest in your people, and implement scalable processes. Then, keep your eyes on the horizon by planning ahead and evolving your recruitment practices to meet the demands of tomorrow.

Because if you want your business to thrive in the long term, you must view growth not as an endpoint but as an ongoing journey, one that requires foresight, agility, and a relentless focus on building a team that can carry your vision forward, no matter what the future holds.

I've outlined the key considerations, and the whole people strategy is a book in itself. Indeed, many have been written about it, mostly dry and boring as fuck. And, if you haven't cottoned on to it yet, you're better off getting the people in place who know how to do all this, rather than spending months or years trying to learn it and perfect it yourself.

Other shit you need to do is:

Embrace a growth mindset. This means viewing every challenge as an opportunity to learn and adapt. When demand spikes, don't just throw more bodies at the problem. You need to invest in systems, processes, and people who can handle scale without breaking.

Invest in technology and automation. The right tools can turn chaos into order. Use applicant tracking systems, CRM platforms, and automation to streamline your recruitment, onboarding, and operational workflows. This frees up your team to focus on strategic initiatives rather than being bogged down in administrative tasks.

Build strategic partnerships. Collaborate with other businesses, industry associations, or even competitors in collaborations. These alliances can open doors to new markets, talent pools, and shared resources, keeping your growth sustainable.

Focus on customer experience and loyalty. Happy customers become your best advocates, providing referrals and repeat business that fuels your growth. Don't neglect your existing clients and customers while chasing new ones.

Maintain financial discipline. Growth can tempt you to overspend or overextend. Keep a close eye on cash flow, margins, and investment returns. Remember: Sustainable growth is about increasing revenue and profitability, not just top-line numbers.

I haven't expanded too much on these areas as they are probably books in themselves. Besides, there are other people who are far more knowledgeable in these areas than I am. Please also see the Further Reading section at the end of this book.

The people strategy, hiring the right people, and building the teams who will achieve your dreams, are most definitely my bag. So, if you'd rather outsource them than go through a lot of trial and error, let's have a chat to see if I'm the right partner for you. I'm not everyone's cup of tea.

Chapter 11
I'm Still Going to Do It All Myself

So, you've read all the advice, nodded sagely at the warnings about burnout and bottlenecks, and you're still determined to handle recruitment and team building yourself. No recruiter, no agency, just you, your business, and a stack of CVs that's about to take over your inbox. Well, hats off to you! There's a certain magic (and madness) in taking the DIY route when it comes to hiring. If you're going to do it, let's make sure you do it brilliantly.

This chapter is your essential guide to running your own recruitment show: how to prepare, what resources you'll need, and the crucial truths you need to know before you dive headfirst into the world of sourcing, screening, and selecting talent solo.

How to Prepare: Mindset, Method, and Motivation

First things first: Recruiting without a recruiter isn't just about posting a job ad and waiting for the perfect candidate to fall into your lap. It takes strategy, stamina, and a willingness to learn as you go. Before you even think about writing that job description, get clear on your why. Are you doing this to save money, to have more control, or because you genuinely want to learn the ropes? Your motivation will shape how you approach every step.

Whatever your motivations, here are my guidelines for how to prepare, followed by my proven 5-step process for solo recruiting:

Set clear objectives. What roles do you need to fill, and why? What does a successful hire look like for your business at this stage? Be ruthless in prioritising what you actually need (not just what sounds impressive on an org chart). Make sure you're recruiting with the long game in mind, not just reactively or in a panic because you suddenly received a big order.

Map out your process. Recruitment is a project, not a one-off task. Plan your timeline, determine who will be involved in decision-making, and outline how you will track candidates and gather feedback. A simple spreadsheet or an affordable applicant tracking system (ATS) can save you hours of chaos down the line.

Brush up on the basics. Even if you're not a recruitment pro, you need to know the essentials: employment law, right-to-work checks, anti-discrimination rules, and how to run a fair and consistent process. A quick online course or a consultation with an HR consultant can help you avoid costly mistakes.

Get ready for the time commitment. Spoiler: Recruitment takes longer than you think. From sifting CVs to arranging interviews and chasing references, be realistic about the hours you'll need to invest and what you might have to put on hold to get it right. Like anything in business or life, you can only achieve the best results if you focus on it. Make a list of all the things you currently do in your business and decide on the two or three things that can be ignored or delegated to someone else for a few weeks or months. The time will depend on the level of role and how many hires you're looking to make.

As a rule of thumb, the time taken to hire for a basic administrator role, if compressed together, will be approximately two to three weeks of your undivided time and attention. The real-time duration, from the point of advertising to somebody starting in the post, is likely to be around three months. This will be significantly longer and more time-consuming for volume, hard-to-find, or senior-level hiring projects. This estimation is also based on the fact that I have nearly thirty years of experience and can do this more efficiently than most. You will need to dedicate much more time to the whole process if you also have to learn how to write compelling adverts, how to interview effectively, about behavioural styles and psychometric profiling, and how to run a recruitment and onboarding process that means you don't make costly hiring mistakes.

Resources You'll Need: Tools, Tactics, and Talent Magnets

Here's the good news: You don't need a recruiter's black book to find great people. With the right tools and tactics, you can run a slick, professional hiring process yourself.

Leverage your network. Tap into your existing contacts, industry peers, and even happy customers. According to LinkedIn, 85% of jobs are filled through networking, and referrals are not only faster to hire but also tend to stay longer. Don't be shy, put the word out!

Use job boards and social media. Post your roles on platforms like Indeed, LinkedIn, and sector-specific job boards. Share your vacancies on your business's social channels and in relevant online groups. A well-crafted post can attract candidates who are already interested in your mission. You can engage some great people if your job adverts are written in a compelling and attractive way. Unfortunately, I see too many job ads that are simply a job description that is cut and pasted into a post or onto a job board. Boring! You will also need to know which job boards work best for certain sectors or skill categories, and how the algorithms work on each one, to maximise the eyes you get on your ad.

My business offers advertising packages for clients who wish to handle the rest of the recruitment process themselves. For more details, please visit www.myrecruitdirect.co.uk.

Remember that when you're advertising a role, it will only be seen by active candidates seeking a new opportunity. That's usually around 15% to 20% of the workforce at any one time. If you suspect that the person you really need in your business is relatively happy in a role and doing great work elsewhere, then you're going to have to dig deeper and conduct a whole territory and talent-mapping exercise, collate contact information, and then make a whole lot of outreach calls and messaging. Unless you engage someone like me.

Create an engaging careers page. Even if it's just a section on your website, make sure you tell your story, showcase your culture, and explain why someone should want to join you. Candidates do their homework, and a strong employer brand can tip the scales in your favour.

Attend industry events and meetups. Whether in person or online, these are goldmines for meeting potential hires in a more relaxed setting. Plus, you'll get a feel for who's genuinely passionate about your sector. There's a fine line here between being a visible and respected operator in your market and getting a reputation for poaching other people's talent. This is one of the reasons why some people use an executive search or headhunt solution.

Develop a talent pool. Keep a running list of interesting people you meet, even if you're not hiring right now. When the time comes, you'll have a warm pipeline to tap into, saving you time and money.

Lean on your team. If you already have employees, involve them in the process. Peer interviews, employee referrals, and honest feedback can help you spot red flags and cultural fit issues early.

This can be a double-edged sword. Imagine your most valued employee recommends their favourite auntie, and you start them as soon as possible. A few months in, you've got issues with Auntie Fave, who hasn't turned up on time once, has made a number of costly mistakes, and has developed an attitude that sets your teeth on edge the second they walk through the door. Totes awks! How do you deal with this without potentially upsetting the working relationship with your star player?

Automate where possible. Use ATS (Applicant Tracking Systems) tools to track applicants, schedule interviews, and send updates. This keeps things organised and ensures no one falls through the cracks.

What You Need to Know: The Realities of DIY Recruitment

Let's not sugar-coat it. Doing your own recruitment is both rewarding and relentless. Here's what you need to know before you commit to the solo path:

Writing a killer job description is half the battle. Be clear about responsibilities, expectations, and what makes your company a great place to work. Avoid jargon and be upfront about any quirks: remote working, dress code, or the fact that you have a dog in the office. The clearer you are, the better your applicant pool will be.

Make sure that you understand who and what your business truly needs for long-term growth and success. Not what you think you need because you're so busy juggling everything that you just want to shed something. Be strategic.

Remember that this job spec is not an advert. The advert should be compelling and tell would-be applicants what's in it for them. Why would they want to come and work for you? Be brutally honest.*

*I advertised for a couple of apprentices a few years ago. The job ad went something along the lines of: "...you will get all the shit jobs, like making the tea and taking the post when it's pissing down with rain..." One of the apprentices bitched and moaned about nearly everything we asked her to do, even when I pointed out the tasks were detailed in the job ad she'd applied for. I also pointed out that we had all done these things as well. My other apprentice was brilliant. He now lives in Sydney, Australia, and has a solid career as a Business Manager with Hays Recruitment.

Screening takes time and discipline. You'll get applications from the brilliant, the bizarre, and the downright baffling. Have a scoring system or checklist to maintain objectivity and consistency. Don't just go with your gut; compare everyone against the same criteria. A seasoned recruiter will often read between the lines of a CV and unearth a diamond in the rough. Not everyone is great at composing a CV, even if they excel in their field. Look at the types of businesses they have worked for. For example, most people who have lasted more than twelve months in a busy transport office will probably be very resilient and great at working under tight deadlines and dealing with people over the phone. Most people who have worked in local authority or public sector roles for a decade or more usually struggle to understand the pace and sense of urgency required in a start-up or rapidly scaling business. Their idea of 'quick and urgent' is not the same as someone who has worked in an entrepreneurial or commercial private sector setting.

Interviews are a two-way street. Interview for the person, not the job role. Ask about what motivates them and find out how they make decisions, what their values are, and what they really want from a role and employer. If you start by telling them all about the company and the role, both parties will be subconsciously asking and responding to fit that brief. Just because somebody can do the job you want them to do doesn't mean that they should. Just because you like them, it doesn't mean that your business, or the job, is going to make them happy and get the best out of them.

Again, I have an online course available that will equip you to conduct effective interviews and avoid making costly hiring mistakes. Take a look at the resources page on www.recruitrecruit.co.uk.

Compliance matters. You must check the right to work in the UK, keep records, and avoid any hint of discrimination. The fines for getting this wrong are eye-watering, and the reputational damage can be worse. I always recommend involving an HR Consultant when you start employing and don't have an in-house resource. I know many fabulous ones around the UK, Ireland (and beyond), and will be happy to make introductions.

Candidate experience is everything. Keep communication prompt and respectful. Even if someone isn't right for you now, a positive experience means they might apply again or recommend you to others. You never know the damage a poor recruitment process can cause.

Several years ago, I interviewed a lovely woman called Jayne. At least, I think it was Jayne; ADHD and menopause are not good bedfellows, and her name may have been something completely different. Anyhow, I was chatting with her about what sort of things she was looking for, and she explained that, even though she had previously worked at a very senior level in HR for a sizable business, she was only looking for something part-time and not particularly taxing. Her situation was that her husband had a thriving business, for which she managed the books. The children she'd largely been a stay-at-home mum for were all off at university or had flown the nest, and she just wanted to do something to get out of the house a bit.

Jayne then told me about a four-stage interview process she'd gone through for a local company for a part-time administrator role. Not only was the interview process completely over-the-top for the level of role, but having attended four interviews (including one with the Managing Director), she never heard from them again. She rang for feedback and got nothing in return. One evening, not long after this crappy experience, Jayne and her husband were out with friends for dinner, and she had a bit of a vent about how unprofessional and impolite it was. Everyone agreed that she'd probably had a narrow escape anyway, if that's the way they treated people.

A few months later, Jayne's friend called her and asked for the name of the company that had treated her so badly. She told him, and he responded, "I thought so. Their submission for a £1.5 million contract we've put out to tender has just landed on my desk...and will be going straight in the bin."

To this day, they probably don't know that their lack of communication with a candidate cost them so dearly.

Don't skip the references. It's tempting to rush, but a quick call to a previous employer can save you a world of pain. Look for patterns, not just glowing reports.

Diversity doesn't happen by accident. If you only hire people who look and think like you, you'll miss out on the creativity and resilience that diverse teams bring. Cast your net wide, challenge your own biases, and prioritise inclusion. It's not some trendy do-gooding bandwagon. Apart from being the ethical thing to do, diversity has been proven time and again to make for more successful, profitable, and resilient businesses.

Know when to ask for help. There's no shame in reaching out to a recruiter, HR consultant, or legal expert if you're out of your depth. Especially for senior or specialist roles, or when you're scaling fast. This also extends to anything remotely compliance-related or legislative in nature. Skimping on professional advice can cost you dearly. If you accidentally blunder something, the fines can be eye-wateringly punitive and destroy your business.

Onboarding is your secret weapon. Once you've found your hire, make them feel welcome and set them up for success. A structured onboarding plan boosts retention and performance from the very start.

Learn as you go. Every hire is a chance to refine your process. Gather feedback, track what worked (and what didn't), and don't be afraid to tweak your approach. Mistakes will be made, and lessons will be learned. People are weird and wonderful, and it is likely that some people will not work out, no matter how well you've handled your recruitment. Some change in personnel as you grow and evolve is not always a bad thing. The important thing is that we recognise when we've missed something that we potentially could have avoided.

Final Thoughts: The DIY Recruitment Adventure

If you're determined to handle recruitment yourself, more power to you. You'll learn more about your business, your team, and your leadership style than you ever thought possible. But remember: Just because you can do it all, doesn't mean you should, especially as your business grows and the stakes get higher. Use every tool, resource, and connection at your disposal. Be methodical, be fair, and be open to learning. And if one day, you decide you want to hand the reins to a recruiter (or even build your own talent team), you'll do so with a deep understanding of what great hiring looks like.

Until then, roll up your sleeves and dive in. The right people are out there. With the right approach and sufficient time dedicated to it, you can find them all on your own.

Conclusion

If you've made it to this point, you're already leagues ahead of most founders – willing to learn, to adapt, and to reflect on what it really takes to build a high-growth business. The truth is, scaling from zero to £30 million (or whatever your dream number is) isn't about luck, unicorn hires, or some secret sauce only the Silicon Valley elite know about. It's about having a clear recruitment strategy, knowing exactly who you need and when, and being brave enough to build a team of brilliant misfits rather than chasing mythical "perfect" candidates.

If there's one lesson that's come up time and again, it's the absolute necessity of having a recruitment strategy from day one. Winging it might get you a couple of decent hires, but it won't build the kind of team that can take your business from scrappy start-up to serious scale-up. Whether you're bootstrapping or flush with investor cash, you need to map out what roles you'll need at each stage, what skills are mission-critical, and (crucially) what kind of personalities will thrive in your unique environment. Don't just hire because you're overwhelmed; hire because you know how this person will move your business forward.

Another hard-won truth: don't be afraid to use professional recruiters, especially in those early, make-or-break stages. The right recruiter isn't just a CV-slinger. They're a strategic partner who'll challenge your assumptions, help you define who you really need (not just what you think you want), and save you from expensive hiring mistakes. Embedding a recruiter into your team, rather than treating them as an external supplier, pays dividends in cultural fit, speed, and long-term retention. And if you're not ready for a full-time hire, don't forget the power of interim talent or outsourcing. Sometimes the best way to fill a fast-evolving role is with someone who can flex and adapt as you figure out what you truly need.

Of course, none of this matters if you don't understand the importance of cultural fit and shared vision. Skills can be taught, but attitude, adaptability, and belief in your mission are non-negotiable. The businesses that scale fastest are those that hire for values and potential, not just for a shiny CV. Be brutally honest about what your culture is, warts and all, and hire people who'll thrive in it, not just survive.

And please, for the love of all things chocolate-coated, don't try to do it all yourself. Yes, you can manage a few hires on your own, but as you grow, the stakes get higher and the process gets messier. Invest in systems and processes early, use technology to keep your recruitment organised, and don't be afraid to ask for help: whether that's a recruiter, a mentor, or your own in-house talent team as you scale.

Finally, remember that building a high-performance team is a journey, not a one-off event. Review your hiring needs regularly, adapt your approach as the business evolves, and continually learn from both successes and setbacks. Celebrate the wins. Especially the small ones, like finally finding that one person who "gets it", and don't let the odd hiring horror story knock you off course.

If you take nothing else from this book, let it be this: The right team, built with intention and care, will take your business further than any single "unicorn" ever could. Remember, the most successful businesses aren't built by lone geniuses or mythical unicorns. They're built by ordinary people who dared to dream big, worked hard, and refused to give up when things got tough.

Build your recruitment strategy, invest in the people who share your vision, and trust that together, you'll build something extraordinary.

As Steve Jobs once said, "Great things in business are never done by one person. They're done by a team of people."

You've got this. Now go out and hire like you mean it.

Next Steps

I've included some suggested reading for those of you who appreciate additional detail and enjoy a good business book to get your commercial cogs turning. They are all available in audio format for those who enjoy listening while commuting or prefer to multitask, such as working out and listening at the same time.

I've uploaded free resources and mini-courses on my websites, and you are welcome to download anything that you find useful:

www.recruitrecruit.co.uk - for start-ups, scale-ups, SME & corporates seeking help with business critical hires and executive search

www.myrecruitdirect.co.uk - for the DIYers out there

www.pyrahharris.co.uk - when you're looking for finance and accountancy bods

Follow me on LinkedIn Sarah Bishop | LinkedIn to see the advice I share in growing your business through people, available training courses and upcoming free webinars, paid masterminds, and ramblings about Vienna, travel, AuDHD, Schnauzers and dogs in general. Whole heap of stuff going on over there that reflects my busy brain!

Want to do it yourself, but aren't sure where to start? You can access short courses through www.recruitrecruit.co.uk on:

- Drafting your strategy and job descriptions
- Writing compelling job advertisements and creating effective job boards and social media campaigns
- How to interview effectively to avoid making costly hiring mistakes
- How to run a robust search and headhunt when advertising isn't bringing you the people you need
- Building effective teams
- What your recruitment process should include
- Offer management, onboarding, and retaining talent

I will also be running some two-day strategy sessions annually for those who want a bit of expert guidance and handholding. You will leave the course with an outlined strategic plan, foundational interview and selection skills, and your questions and concerns answered. Additionally, you will have your own hiring playbook to take away and follow. Full details are to be confirmed, and spaces will be limited to ensure that everyone gets appropriate time and attention. To join the waiting list and receive updates on dates, locations, full content, and pricing, visit www.recruitrecruit.co.uk/Scale-up-mailing-list and complete the short form.

If you've read this and thought, "I want to get the professionals in to make sure I get this right, and this weirdo seems like my cup of tea!" Then let's have a chat. Perhaps even a spot of lunch. You can email me at sarah@recruitrecruit.co.uk or, if you want me to be properly equipped with an idea of where you're at before we have a conversation, then please complete this short questionnaire:

Further Reading

There is a plethora of reading material available to help you grow your business. Some try to cover all aspects of business growth, and others focus on narrower topics. Whilst I am very much a life-long learner and like to understand many different facets of business and life, I also realise that there is only so much time and so much life! That's why getting people who are better at certain things into our business, and letting them take the lead in that area, will allow you to achieve so much more than you can flying solo. Even if you decide that you don't want the responsibility of employees, the same principles can be applied to choosing your outsourced partners and freelancers.

For those who love to delve more deeply into everything, here's a curated further reading list of 20 books that will deepen your understanding of building teams, scaling through people, recruitment strategy, and the real-world challenges of growing a business. Each one echoes the themes and practical wisdom woven throughout this book:

1. *The E-Myth Revisited* by Michael E. Gerber
   A must-read on why most small businesses don't work and what to do about it, with a strong focus on building systems and thinking beyond the founder.

2. *Who Not How* by Dan Sullivan & Dr. Benjamin Hardy
   A game-changer for shifting from "How do I do this?" to "Who can do this for me?" This is essential reading for any founder learning to build a team.

3. *Good to Great* by Jim Collins
   A classic on what separates truly great companies from the merely good, with deep insights into leadership and people decisions.

4. *TeamWork* by Natalie Dawson
   Packed with practical advice on hiring, onboarding, and scaling teams that perform at a high level.

5. *The Five Dysfunctions of a Team* by Patrick Lencioni
   A leadership fable that uncovers the root causes of team failure and how to build trust and accountability.

6. *Scaling Up* by Verne Harnish
   A comprehensive guide to growing your business, with a strong focus on people, strategy, execution, and cash.

7. *High Growth Handbook* by Elad Gil
   Real-world advice for navigating the challenges of hypergrowth, including hiring, culture, and organisational change.

8. *Traction: Get a Grip on Your Business* by Gino Wickman
   A practical framework for building a business that runs smoothly. This is especially useful for founders ready to scale their teams.

9. *The Dream Manager* by Matthew Kelly
   Explores how supporting your employees' personal dreams can transform engagement and retention.

10. *Radical Candor* by Kim Scott
    A modern classic on how to build a culture of honest feedback and care, critical for start-up and scale-up teams.

11. *Drive: The Surprising Truth About What Motivates Us* by Daniel H. Pink
    A deep dive into what really motivates people at work and vital reading for any leader building a team.

12. *First, Break All the Rules* by Marcus Buckingham & Curt Coffman
    Based on research from Gallup, this book reveals what the world's best managers do differently when building teams.

13. *The Culture Code* by Daniel Coyle
    An exploration of the secrets behind highly successful teams and how to foster belonging, trust, and high performance.

14. *No Rules Rules: Netflix and the Culture of Reinvention* by Reed Hastings & Erin Meyer
    A behind-the-scenes look at how Netflix built a culture of freedom and responsibility.

15. *101 Team Building Exercises* by Herman Otten
    A hands-on resource for improving communication, trust, and collaboration within teams.

16. *Elevate Your Team* by Robert Glazer
    Actionable strategies for building a high-performance, growth-focused team culture.

17. *Leaders Eat Last* by Simon Sinek
    Explores the importance of servant leadership and building teams that feel safe and inspired.

18. *Multipliers: How the Best Leaders Make Everyone Smarter* by Liz Wiseman
    How great leaders amplify the intelligence and capability of those around them.

19. *The Making of a Manager* by Julie Zhuo
    A practical guide for new managers on building and leading effective teams as your business grows.

20. *Reinventing Organizations* by Frederic Laloux
    A visionary look at how organisations can be structured for purpose, self-management, and people-centric growth.

Each of these books offers a different lens on the art and science of building teams, scaling through people, and avoiding the common pitfalls that trip up even the most promising start-ups. Happy reading and happy building!

www.ingramcontent.com/pod-product-compliance
Lightning Source LLC
Chambersburg PA
CBHW070954120726
47910CB00004B/1232

* 9 7 8 1 0 6 8 1 8 8 7 0 1 *